Water Politics
Continuity and Change

Helen Ingram

Foreword by
Congressman Morris K. Udall

UNIVERSITY OF NEW MEXICO PRESS
Albuquerque

In memory of Dean F. Peterson

The first edition of this book acknowledged a debt to Congressman Morris K. Udall, who in 1967 opened his files to scholarly investigation. The author gratefully acknowledges continued debts to the congressman and to Steve Reynolds, New Mexico state engineer. Both instructed a political scientist from different perspectives about the real world of water politics.

In revising this edition of the book, I was assisted by a research grant from the Ford Foundation.

Library of Congress Cataloging in Publication Data

Ingram, Helen M., 1937–
    Water politics : continuity and change / Helen Ingram.
    p.   cm.
    Rev. ed. of: Patterns of politics in water resource development. 1969.
    Includes bibliographical references.
    ISBN 0-8263-1189-X. — ISBN 0-8263-1190-3 (pbk.)
    1. Water resources development—Government policy—New Mexico. I. Ingram, Helen M., 1937– Patterns of politics in water resource development. II. Title.
HD1694.N615   1990
333.91′009789—dc20   89-70524
                                     CIP

Cover design by Michael Reed

This volume is an updated and revised version of
Patterns of Politics in Water Resource Development:
A Case Study of New Mexico's Role in
the Colorado River Basin Bill
(Albuquerque: University of New Mexico
Division of Government Research, 1969).

Contents

Foreword

Congressman Morris K. Udall

Enactment of the Colorado River Basin Project Act in 1968 was a milestone. By authorizing construction of the Central Arizona Project (CAP), the act was a giant step in Arizona's long quest to use its share of the waters of the Colorado River. More significantly, as this book makes clear, it marked a turning point in the politics of western water development.

In the 1930s, 1940s, and 1950s, the federal government built, or committed itself to build, big dams and irrigation projects on nearly every major river system in the arid West. In the eyes of Congress and the Executive Branch and, perhaps to a lesser extent, the general public, big water projects were almost by definition good for the country. However, the social, political, and economic upheavals of the 1960s, which wrought great changes in our attitudes toward government, the environment, and ourselves, also changed the attitudes toward water development. These changes in turn resulted in new people and groups emerging and altering the dynamics of water development.

In her 1969 book *Pattern of Politics in Water Resource Development: The Role of New Mexico in the Colorado River Basin Bill,* Helen Ingram skillfully examined the interplay of issues, interests, and personalities that produced the compromises that enabled the bill to pass. Among other things, her examination found New Mexico's role in the process to reflect an unraveling of the political consensus that had been the foundation of the dam-building era. At the time, however, it was not clear how or whether the elements of that old consensus would be rearranged. The future was, as it usually is, in doubt. Now, twenty years later, Ms. Ingram has updated that analysis of the nascent trends in water development. This new work, *Water Politics: Continuity and Change,* offers fresh insight into the evolving dynamics of western water policy.

I have been privileged to serve in Congress as a representative from the state of Arizona since 1961 and have been involved in the passage of the 1968 act. In considering its aftermath, I can attest that the contours of today's political landscape validate Ms. Ingram's original analysis. The old unanimity on water projects is dead. Concerns for the environment and federal budget deficits weigh far more heavily today on the thinking of elected officials than they did in 1968. I highly doubt that CAP legislation could be passed in today's Congress.

Enactment of the National Environmental Policy Act (NEPA) in 1969 set the stage for the current era of water politics. In that act, Congress required that any proposed federal action be studied to identify its environmental impacts, appropriate mitigation of adverse impacts, and alternative actions available. It also required consideration of public comment on any proposal or alternatives. This environmental impact study (EIS) process has become a crucial element in government decision making, providing grounds for making changes in project proposals or for killing them.

For the Central Arizona Project, the NEPA process resulted in exhaustive and extremely valuable studies of the state's flora and fauna. This information in turn led to a host of changes in the project's design to mitigate adverse impacts on wildlife, plants, and aesthetic sensibilities. Although the cost of the studies and changes will ultimately be close to $200 million of the project's estimated $3.5 billion total cost, there is little argument that they greatly enhanced the CAP and the environment and are well worth the expense. NEPA also figured in the most recent change in the CAP. In 1985, litigation brought by a national coalition of environmental groups challenging the adequacy of the EIS on the proposed Cliff Dam on the Verde River was a key element in the delegation's decision the following year to drop the dam in return for support for continued funding to complete remaining features of the project.

By the end of the 1960s, as the federal government's financial condition worsened, Congress found it much harder to justify authorizing and funding major new water projects or any other activities that required federal subsidies. Political gridlock delayed any new projects from being enacted until 1986, when congress passed an omnibus bill authorizing new construction for the Corps of Engineers. That bill established as new federal policy that local beneficiaries of a project must share in the costs—up-front. Along with the need to pass environmental muster, this cost-sharing requirement is a major hurdle for any new project, especially a large one. The net effect has been fewer new projects being proposed and those that are tend to be smaller, multipurpose ones.

As it was affected by NEPA, so too was the Central Arizona Project affected by the federal government's money woes. Once construction began in 1972, obtaining appropriations sufficient to maintain even a minimum rate of construction became an annual battle for the congressional delegation. By 1985 the project was still less than 50 percent complete, and it was clear that unless Arizona climbed aboard the cost-sharing bandwagon, the CAP wouldn't be complete until well after the year 2000. After lengthy negotiations, local interests agreed to contribute roughly $300 million to speed construction of the project's features. Since the signing of this so-called Plan 6 agreement and the decision to drop Cliff Dam, federal appropriations for CAP have continued at record levels. Completion of the main aqueduct to Tucson is now scheduled for late 1991, and most remaining project features should be finished by the mid-1990s.

As it has evolved from concept to concrete, the Central Arizona Project has reflected our changing national conditions. Changing demographics have caused it to become less an agricultural water supply project and more a municipal and industrial water supply project for the Phoenix and Tucson metropolitan areas. Environmental concerns caused its initially planned power source—Colorado River dams—to be eliminated in exchange for a coal-fired power plant—Navajo Generating Station. Similar concerns led to the elimination of Orme and Cliff dams on the Salt and Verde rivers. New Mexico's dam on the Gila River may never be built. NEPA studies altered CAP's design, inflation increased its costs, and the government's changing financial fortunes caused Arizona to bear a greater cost of construction. Despite these changes, however, the basic purpose of the Colorado River Basin Act remains intact: to enable Arizona to utilize fully her entitlement to Colorado River water.

With the completion of the CAP, Arizona will become fully immersed in a new era, one that will be defined by how her citizens determine what it will mean for Arizona "to utilize fully" her share of the river. State government, city councils, Indian tribes, farmers, miners, environmentalists, and academics are increasingly wrestling with issues involving water allocation, water transfer, groundwater recharge, water marketing, water quality, water shortages, and the like. Efficient, wise management will be the hallmark of this new era, not only for Arizona, but also for the federal government. For its part, the Bureau of Reclamation last year announced that its primary mission would no longer be construction of new projects; instead, it will emphasize improving the operation and maintenance of existing projects.

Among the most challenging issues facing Arizona and the federal government is the need to settle the outstanding water rights claims of Arizona Indian tribes. In this regard, the CAP has proven far more useful than perhaps anyone envisioned in 1968. Colorado River water allocations and the CAP delivery system have been essential elements in negotiated claims settlement agreements, which have quantified tribal water rights and provided cash for their development. Through such agreements, which require authorizing legislation and appropriations from Congress, tribes have converted "paper rights" into "wet water" and thus acquired the means crucial to their economic development and well-being.

CAP water and the CAP delivery system have been critical elements in these settlements, providing negotiators great flexibility in structuring multiparty agreements. Through hard work and its 1978 settlement, the first in Arizona, the Ak-Chin Indian Community has become essentially self-sustaining. The Tohono O'Odham (Papago) hope to achieve similar gains from their 1982 settlement once their CAP water deliveries begin in the early 1990s. The Salt River–Pima-Maricopa Indian Community's settlement, enacted in 1988, is expected to make the community a major economic force in the Phoenix area for generations to come. Currently, negotiations are either under way or are contemplated to attempt to settle the claims of the Indians of the Fort McDowell, Gila River, and San Carlos Apache reservations. Use of CAP water and the CAP delivery system will undoubtedly play a key role in the settlement of these claims.

Each succeeding generation of political leaders faces a different agenda of issues and problems that reflect their times. The complex fabric of new issues overlaying old ones, the ever-changing mix of personalities and priorities within our political institutions and social organizations—all this makes for fascinating study. Just as the Colorado River Basin Act shifted our focus from authorization to appropriations, so is the imminent completion of the CAP system giving rise to an array of new questions: once we have established our water supplies, how will we manage them? What are the wisest, the best, the fairest ways?

To participate actively and constructively in scholarly and political discussion and debate over the answers to these questions is a challenge to all students of public policy, and to all citizens. With *Water Politics: Continuity and Change*, Helen Ingram has addressed this challenge in a compelling and eminently readable way. I appreciate and commend her effort.

Congressman Morris K. Udall
and Helen Ingram.
Photo by Judy Lensink.

1

Patterns of Politics in Water Resources: Continuity and Change

Justification

The centerpiece of this book, a case study of the role of New Mexico in the passage of the Colorado River Basin Act, (CRBA), recounted in chapters 2 through 8, was written in the mid-1960s. The legislation was a landmark of western water development, but also, like the last of the dinosaurs, an anachronism. The Central Arizona Project (CAP), authorized by the law, is now commonly considered to close out further big construction works that poured millions of federal dollars into providing cheap and abundant water for growing farms and cities in the seventeen western states. Numerous delays have slowed completion into the mid-1990s of the much-modified and overbudget CAP. As the Afterword in chapter 9 chronicles, one of the two companion projects slated for New Mexico was scrapped while financing of the other continues to be the focus of fierce debate. Common wisdom now says that the water development era is past, and that water conservation, reallocation, and transfer have superseded the provision of new supplies through dams and aqueducts.

With the eclipse of monumental federal projects, the actors who made their political livelihood in the water business have gone on to other things, retired, or died. Arizona's Carl Hayden, the Democratic dean of the Senate, retired shortly after the signing of the legislation, pleased to cap his list of legislative accomplishments with the passage of the Colorado River Basin Act. Congressman Morris K. Udall, Democrat from southern Arizona who performed as core activist for the Central Arizona Project and thereby attracted the enmity of environmental groups, subsequently built a career as an environmentally sensitive legislator, winning particular accolades for shepherding the Alaska wilderness and parks legislation through the gauntlet of Capitol Hill. Looking back (in a somewhat nostalgic joint appearance with his brother Stuart in 1987), he expressed doubts publicly as to whether he would be in favor of the Central Arizona Project were he to relive that part of his career.[1] Democratic chair of the Committee on Interior and Insular Affairs, Wayne Aspinall, was retired from his

1

congressional seat on the western slope of Colorado through electoral defeat. Few figures important to the case study reported in this book are still movers in water politics in the late 1980s.

Of what interest is a twenty-year-old study likely to be to the contemporary reader? Water has a strong emotional attachment, and people battling over control of water perform intricate and imaginative political maneuvers. The making of the Colorado River basin legislation is a fascinating story. Dramatic elements exist, including high stakes such as the future of development in the West and the flooding of irreplaceable wilderness canyons; and there are plenty of heroes and villains. The story is especially well supplied with skillful political actors. It is difficult to read the pages that follow without both admiring the political agility with which Congressman Morris K. Udall constructs agreements among disparate interests and feeling sympathy when the carefully constructed coalitions come apart repeatedly. The brilliance with which the New Mexico state engineer Steve Reynolds protected the water interests of his state as he saw those interests is certain to provoke envy among citizens of other states less well served. The sprouts of the contemporary environmental movement peek through in the mobilization and media strategies pursued by David Brower and his Sierra Club lieutenants in defeating the Grand Canyon dams and defending wilderness along the Gila River.

It is impossible to discern where we are going in water policy until we understand where we have been, and the history told in this volume is solid ground from which to interpret current events. The nature of the water problem and the goals of the water policy are apparently no longer the same. The machinery for policy making appears to have been shifted to lower levels of government and to private enterprise. A new vocabulary drawn from economics has been introduced. Which lessons from the past still apply? Recall the old saw that water flows downhill except when it is flowing uphill toward money. A standard for sorting out what is constant from what is changing would clearly be useful.

The analysis of the patterns of politics as they operated to produce the Colorado River Basin Act of 1968 is a fixed point at the apex of reclamation politics. The legislation was important, and the reclamation politics that produced it followed classic patterns. Since the study was made and first published before the changes of the 1970s and 1980s, the analysis is not distorted by hindsight of what was to come. The inevitable temptation for the analyst to select from past events those aspects that verify his or her interpretations cannot operate here. Instead, the CRBA offers a benchmark against which to compare events that developed, unaffected by the revisionism associated with looking backward.

Standards of Measure

Revisiting the water politics and policy evidenced in the Colorado River

Basin Act raises the clear question of appropriate standards against which meaningful change should be measured. In the terminology of policy analysis, evaluators must choose which available indicators are most significant. Changes in policy design, including policy objectives, bureaucratic relationships, and the choice of tools to motivate target populations may be tracked. For instance, laws may add water conservation and environmental quality as objectives. Or, water rates and tax increases may take the place of subsidies and large-scale construction as policy tools to allocate water. Alternatively, it is possible to focus on policy outputs, such as expenditures or numbers of new project starts. Change can also be measured in terms of policy outcomes as experienced by people and imposed upon the physical environment. Among the possible consequences, the configuration of beneficiaries and losers from water policy may be altered.

Meaningful change can also be evaluated by asking what difference reforms have made. Using a 1960s case study as a benchmark provides grounds to measure improvement. Water policy, welfare, education, juvenile justice, and various other issues have sharpened the knives of critics and whetted the reformers' appetites. For example, in 1971 the president's National Water Commission urged that "beneficiaries pay" be the rule for financing water projects, including reallocations. It was argued that projects would become more efficient and that fewer unnecessary allocations of resources would be made than under the old system in which the federal government provided handsome subsidies. With such reforms at least partially in place in the late 1980s, it is possible to measure what and how much change has resulted.

Chapter 3 identifies a model of what the author in the mid-1960s believed to be the pattern of politics in water. The key factors in the model included (a) perceptions of the issue and relevant stakes, (b) actors, and (c) arenas and decision rules. The larger view of water resources politics and policy since the original model more than twenty years ago allows for a more authoritative evaluation of the model and which factor or factors exert the most influence.

Overview of the Book

Measuring the change of water policy and politics since the benchmark of the Colorado River Basin Act is the task of the remainder of this chapter. After identifying those attributes of water politics and policy that have remained stable, the pattern of politics at the time of the Colorado River Basin Act is contrasted with the pattern that has evolved. Particular attention is paid to identifying winners and losers and how influence has shifted from the 1960s to the 1990s. The final section of the chapter assesses the extent of change that has actually occurred in water policy and the adequacy of models, including the political model set out in this book and those espoused by water reformers to capture and explain events.

Chapter 2 is an exercise in problem definition. It argues that the Colorado River basin legislation is understandable only in political terms since it makes little sense either economically or in hydrologic terms. The political model through which the pattern of politics as it operated in the 1960s can be understood is introduced in chapter 3. The shortcomings of political science approaches to policy in the 1960s are revealed in that the model is preoccupied with process rather than policy content. The contemporary policy scholar's commitment to identifying means for policy improvement rather than simply understanding is almost wholly lacking. More recent literature is not cited. As an abstract portrayal of reclamation politics in the big development era, however, the model retains its original value as an exceptionally accurate portrayal and has therefore not been substantially revised.

Chapter 4 introduces the case to which the model is applied. It describes in broad terms the initiation, formulation, and passage of the Colorado River Basin Act. Major actors are introduced and their perspectives explored. The relationships of these actors to one another in building and blocking support for various aspects of the bill are examined. The conditions finally achieved for successful passage of the bill are identified.

New Mexico assumes the leading role in chapters 5 through 7 which focus on the two projects at stake for that state in the legislation. In chapter 5 the Animas–La Plata Project is treated as an example of typical reclamation politics. The more extraordinary history of the authorization of Hooker Dam is separated into two parts. In chapter 6 the negotiations between New Mexico and Arizona for new water for New Mexico are examined. Chapter 7 describes the environmentalist challenge to Hooker Dam, and the way that challenge was handled in the political process. Chapter 8 reproduces the author's original overview and assessment as it was published in 1969. Chapter 9 provides an afterword which recounts the course of events affecting the projects written about in the original study.

Continuities

The key factors driving the politics of water resources in the 1960s are identified in chapter 4. From the perspective of the time, the pattern of politics appeared very stable. While challenges were evident, most of the important interests got what they wanted from the system and opponents were either bought out or excluded. Events have shown the system to be a good deal more flexible than anticipated and the pattern of politics in water has undergone considerable change. Some of the factors originally described have remained very strong while others have become much less important and have been exchanged for different influences. Even the constants in water policy require restatement because the author's understanding has been deepened and refined over twenty years of additional observation.

Social Value of Water

The perception of water as a special resource with important symbolic and emotional value is a persistent factor that underlies past and emerging patterns of politics in water. As chapter 3 indicates, water is believed to have the Midas touch, assuring a prosperous future for whatever communities have it. As is the case with wishes granted, it is difficult for a community to envision having sufficient dependable supply. Water availability is viewed as being a limit to possibilities, and communities would prefer that limits be placed very far out.

Perhaps because so little attention was paid in the 1960s to efficiency of water allocations, the original study made no distinction between attachment to water for economic reasons and broader community concerns. Increasing focus on economic values of water has made it clearer that people's attachment to water goes well beyond expectations of financial return. For instance, a survey of Arizona farmers in the early 1980s found that agriculturalists with land closest to the Central Arizona Project aqueduct, who might reasonably expect the greatest benefit from the project, were not necessarily the most supportive. Instead, interviewers discovered "the strength of the farmers' emotional commitment to the project seems to vary directly with the degree to which they feel threatened about their future." A respondent expressed his view, "Price doesn't matter. The point is we need more water. It is our last chance." [2]

Water still symbolizes such values as opportunity, security, and self-determination. Water represents these values less because the water itself has economic value than because control over it signals social organization and political power. [3] A sense of lineage and inheritance are among the emotions stirred by control over water. Strong communities are able to hold on to their water and put it to work. Communities that lose control over their water probably will fail in trying to control much else of importance. Most areas from which water has been transferred have viewed the loss of water as an impoverishing event and resisted the transfer even when economic compensation to the owners of water rights is involved. Loss of water carries negative consequences to tax base, community infrastructure, ability to attract and hold residents, and to governing institutions. [4]

Particularly in poor rural communities, such as upper Rio Grande Hispanic villages and Indian tribes, water is bound up with culture and way of life. Water also seems to be perceived as an integral part of urban lifestyle in a desert environment. While urban water officials in desert cities engage in preachments of conservation, there is real resistance to accepting natural water availability as a limit to community choices related to growth. [5] Thus, the perception of water as a special social resource has not changed since the 1960s.

Water as a Local Resource

Chapter 3 observes that water is seen as a local resource, an observation that would seem to hold anywhere. After studying seven irrigation districts in the U.S. and Spain, Maass and Anderson concluded that locals place great value on control and have to a remarkable extent succeeded in protecting their autonomy. Locals continue to pursue their own values even in defiance of national policies that are supposed to accompany national money if these policies are a serious threat to local custom.[6] Communities still plan in terms of *our* water, assuming other communities will do the same. Even when laws mandate the consideration of river basins and hydrologic systems, implementation tends to protect localized interests. For instance, the Arizona State Groundwater Management Act of 1980 establishes Active Management Areas (AMAs) where overdraft is occurring, sets the target of safe yield in aquifers, and requires new developers to prove the availability of 100 years' supply. Cities within AMAs have reacted by buying groundwater rights in areas outside AMAs where no safe yield requirement is imposed, thereby simply transferring and obscuring the overdraft. Despite the fact that Doña Ana County in New Mexico and the city of El Paso share a common river system and several aquifers, these neighbors could not be further apart in terms of water planning. The city of El Paso has been trying for some years to externalize the problems of its rising demand and limited supply by acquiring water rights in New Mexico rather than negotiating with adjacent farmers in Texas. For their part, lower Rio Grande basin residents in New Mexico appear to think that any water use in New Mexico should come before any need in El Paso and have done everything in their power to block the transfers. The perception of water as a local resource becomes, if anything, more firmly held as competition for water increases.

Hidden or Displaced Costs

It is a well-accepted axiom in public policy studies that the quality of policy decisions can be related to the availability of information and the access of affected interests to decision-making processes.[7] The best decisions are made when the interests that potentially bear burdens and enjoy benefits are informed and participate. Judged by the criteria of information and access, water resources policy continues to be flawed by hidden costs and unrepresented but affected interests. The full economic costs of water projects during the development era were disguised by subsidized loans with long repayment periods, unrealistically low interest rates, and charges based upon ability to pay. Present and future taxpayers represented too diffuse and unorganized an interest to participate. Similarly, the adverse environmental impacts of overdevelopment and management of water were slighted. As the case study to follow indicates, environmen-

6

talists could be stirred to action when parks and wilderness areas were at stake, but the larger ecological impacts of concentrated water development failed to rank high on the agenda of environmental groups.

In demographic terms a great tipping of the continent has occurred, with population slipping away from centers in the Northeast and Midwest to resettle in the Sun Belt. Natural river basins and aquifers have been made to accommodate dramatic increases in population through large-scale transfers of water from one basin to another and overdrafting of groundwater. Water policy has also facilitated the movement of agricultural production and investment by subsidizing delivery of irrigation supplies to warm, dry areas with long growing seasons such as the Imperial Valley. Such modifications of natural systems are not without physical consequences. The eminent geographer Gilbert F. White has noted that attention to technical solutions to problems related to the Colorado River compounds difficulties to society through unintended consequences. [8] The increases of salinity in the lower Colorado and evidences of selenium poisoning of water supplies to wildlife and people provide testimony to this effect. Adequate policy analysis could uncover many hidden costs but, at least in water policy, determination to acquire short-term, immediate gains continues to take precedence over anticipation of unexpected problems.

Closed Politics

Policy-making coalitions in water resources politics still tend to be small, stable, and exclusive. The major participants in the politics of water have had interest, skill, and resources. They are associated with the big water users including municipalities, agribusiness, energy, and industry. Expertise is a key resource and it is necessary to have the appropriate credentials, preferably engineering, and to speak the water jargon to participate fully. The Colorado River basin legislation was a water development spectacular, and yet the cast of characters reflected a tight circle of interests with a direct stake. Environmentalists, or conservationists, as they were called at the time, forced their way into decision making to protect the Grand Canyon and the Gila Wilderness. While they accomplished some of their limited aims, they were never really dealt into the game.

The historian Donald Worster believes that there is a relationship between intensive water development and concentration of power in the hands of the few. For him, dams and ditches have not so much built the West as torn down frontier democracy. [9] Other authors with different perspectives have also observed the closed forums within which water policy is made. Water politics has been described in terms of iron triangles of mutually reinforcing relationships between benefiting constituencies, congressional committees, and federal agencies. [10] Philip Fradkin has called the Colorado the "White Man's River," or more narrowly, the "Anglo River." He writes:

7

Even within this last concentric racial circle, the river has been divided and diverted by only a very small segment of Caucasian society. Others do benefit, but only the few distribute the water. This small group of decision makers and technicians has been invariably white, Anglo, male, and extremely conscious of how they wanted the economic benefits of water dispersed. Few others have taken the time or interest to understand or deal with the esoteric and arcane world of water law and politics. [11]

Robert Gottlieb terms the obscure group that controls water decisions "the water industry" and describes it as little known to the public or press and communicating to each other in a technically dense and often inaccessible language. [12]

It is rare for water supply issues to become the basis of broadly based conflict within localities because interests in water are differentiated along geographic rather than ideological or partisan lines. Gottlieb and others have noted that water quality and toxic pollution of drinking water supply have mobilized strong grassroots constituencies in a number of communities that are capable of challenging water industry control. The more common pattern is for special interests to negotiate their differences over water without precipitating a public debate. The Arizona Groundwater Management Act of 1980 came out of a rump group that involved the governor, a handful of legislators, and spokespersons for the key user groups including cities, the mines, and agriculture. Environmentalists have made no more than symbolic inroads into the inner sanctum of decision making concerning water quantity.

Patterns of politics in water have been constantly characterized by enormous pressure for agreement and a united front among interests. In the face of challenge the small, stable coalitions controlling water decisions react either by co-optation or by exclusion. One environmentalist holding a position of token representation on a board representing mainly user interests referred to the power of the "flake" factor. Environmentalists were dismissed by others as flakes willing to make trouble for its own sake unless they proved otherwise by reasonable, moderate stands on issues. For that reason, environmentalists felt subtle pressure to avoid conflict unless there was some chance of victory. [13]

Era of Big Federal Projects

It would be repetitive to detail the way in which the enduring characteristics of water politics were evidenced during the era of large-scale water development. The legislative history of New Mexico's role in the Colorado River basin legislation in chapters 2 through 8 provides a classic portrayal. An outline of the key features will suffice.

1. Social values relating water to security and opportunity were pursued

through the acquisition of new water provided by federal projects. When new water was made available to serve existing, expanding, and new needs, no present user faced the insecurity of having to cut back. The local economy received an infusion of new jobs through construction and the community felt an optimism about future limitless possibilities.

2. The federal level was the focal arena because of its breadth of jurisdiction, comprehending entire river basins. The federal level also had the advantages of superior expertise in the construction agencies and major funding capacity.

3. As locally based political actors with access to the federal arena, members of Congress played a key role. The House and Senate Interior committees, which overrepresented constituencies in the West with a keen interest in water projects and served various congressional constituencies, were strung together by a process of log rolling in which political feasibility counted for more than engineering or financing.

4. Federal agencies were also closely tied to local constituencies. The Bureau of Reclamation set aside its mission to help settle the West with small farmers and spread agrarian democracy in order to serve local elites including established, entrepreneurial agriculturalists and contractors. (In some cases federal agencies were adept in expanding local support for projects that were at first backed by fairly weak and narrow interests. The interests of large-scale bureaucracy were protected by evaluative criteria that gave the edge to high-technology solutions to water problems.)

5. Local interests, while appealing to the federal level for help, continued to dominate most water decisions. In the process of implementation, federal rules and timetables unpopular at the local level were set aside in favor of locally preferred ways of doing things.

Winners and Losers in the Era of Big Federal Projects

While the type of politics in water resources is commonly termed "distributive," that is, where only benefits and no costs are perceived,[14] it is reasonable to suppose that the benefits and costs of water development are distributed somewhat differently in practice than was anticipated by the enabling legislation. Just how much original goals have become displaced is seldom a matter of official record. Postproject construction evaluation studies are rare in water resources. Further, even if one knew whether or not the legislation met its goals, it would be difficult to say for sure whether any particular interest would have fared better or worse under alternative or no legislation. Despite the shortcomings of the evidence, it is nonetheless possible to broadly assess whether the content of policy was compatible with the core values of various interests. Judged by this criterion, there were some clear winners and losers during the development era.

9

Winners

1. Growth interests in localities receiving construction benefits. Project construction meant jobs, and plentiful water fueled expansion and development with attendant building, real estate, and banking booms. Irrigated lands became more valuable because they could produce more than dry lands. In his book *Water and Power*, William Kahrl contrasts the water-driven wealth of Los Angeles with the poverty of Owens Valley, arguing that control of water allocations meant great prosperity for Los Angeles and loss of control resulted in stagnation for Owens Valley. [15] Some analysts have argued that localities should have examined the benefits more carefully and questioned what burdens were associated with federal subsidies to projects. [16] While local taxpayers and the environment may have suffered in the long run, many direct beneficiaries profited a great deal. Worster argues that benefits of water development are far from evenly distributed and that water development has facilitated vast accumulations of wealth and power. [17]

2. Locally based policy actors. Brilliant administrative and political careers have been built upon successful negotiations in water development politics. William Mulholland and Joseph Lippincott established legendary reputations as water administrators in California. B. A. Fowler and John Orme played key roles in establishing the Salt River Project in Arizona. State engineer of New Mexico Steve Reynolds, one of the principals in the case study to follow, has established for himself and for the state an international reputation for rational allocation of resources. Solons such as Robert S. Kerr, Clinton P. Anderson, Hayden, Aspinall, and Udall could not have pursued their illustrious careers without having paid dues to their states or districts through procuring water projects. Some great water czars remain. Congressman Jamie Whitten, chairman of the House Appropriations Committee, is a zealous supporter of traditional water policy. In 1985 he celebrated the opening of the Tennessee-Tombigbee Waterway by floating down the canal on a flower-bedecked barge. [18]

3. Construction bureaucracies. There is no question that water has been the political basis of large and important federal bureaucracies, including the Army Corps of Engineers, Bureau of Reclamation, Soil Conservation Service, and the construction program in the Environmental Protection Agency. Analysts differ about the relative influence of agencies and local constituencies in water choices. There is some evidence that localities warped their own preferences in order to fit the evaluative criteria of the Bureau of Reclamation that preferred engineering feats and good benefit/cost ratios to medium-level technology projects responsive to immediate local needs. On the other hand, the Bureau of Reclamation put the implementation of the 160-acre limitation on the back burner because it was offensive to local farmers with large

landholdings.

Clarke and McCool performed an analysis of seven federal natural resource agencies and concluded that the powerful agencies, termed "superstars," are capable of sustaining themselves even in the face of changing national priorities and lessening local support for traditional missions.[19] The characterization, they conclude, does not hold for the Bureau of Reclamation, which is called a "shooting star," because its fortunes turned down sharply in the 1960s. In his book *Cadillac Desert*, Marc Reisner blames the beginning of the bureau's troubles on Commissioner Floyd Dominy, who was adept at pursuing bureaucratic aims during the reclamation era, but refused to recognize changing realities.[20] The chapters that follow evidence some of this blindness on the part of the bureau.

Losers

1. Other higher value federal investments. Reclamationists argued the water projects were in the national economic interest because they were socially desirable and also paid their own way. Actually, water development represented a considerable federal outlay, and monies spent were therefore not available for other investment. People in localities receiving the benefit did not pay the cost. Reclamation development was characterized by disassociation of beneficiaries from payment burdens through subsidies, long repayment periods, repayment through development funds generated by hydropower users, and mineral revenues. Economists have repeatedly pointed out that many projects have been built that made no positive contribution to national economic efficiency. The interest of the federal taxpayer tended to be broad and unfocused and not well represented at the federal level. To some extent the parsimonious attitude of the old Bureau of the Budget toward many water projects in the development era represented this perspective, but as the chapters that follow illustrate, the bureau was often ineffective.

2. Environmentalists and future generations. There were examples, such as the one recounted in this book, where environmentalists stopped or fundamentally altered projects during the development era. However, for every Grand Canyon and Echo Park saved, dozens of projects with adverse environmental impacts on less well known natural areas were approved. For instance, water development has led to the flooding of irreplaceable canyons such as Glen, made famous, after it was inundated, by the Sierra Club book *The Place No One Knew*. Too often water has been developed and overused, causing unnecessary levels of environmental deterioration. Waterlogging, the result of the outflow of surface irrigation works, has caused drainage problems and buildup of salts and toxics in both ground- and surface waters. Premature use and siltation of irreplaceable reservoir sites is a major problem in intergen-

erational terms. The failure to respect limits and hydrologic realities has resulted in enormous overdrafts of water in many areas, which bequeath to future generations a harmed resouce. In addition, interbasin transfer projects fueled development and population expansion in environmentally sensitive areas.

Environmentalists during the development era did not even try to block the bulk of environmentally damaging water decisions. In 1971, a longtime staff member of the Sierra Club said that in the past the organization had not objected to 90 percent of water projects.[21] Unless a water project directly threatened a park or wilderness area, environmentalists absented themselves from the decision-making area. Further, as Dean Mann observed, conservation groups simply "took a walk" after their narrow specific interest had been accommodated, that is, no dams in the Grand Canyon, and did not stay involved in policy making to mitigate more general environmental harm.[22]

3. Disadvantaged peoples. Only a few people were able to play the federal water projects game to their advantage and many others were left out. Indians, Hispanics, blacks, and other poor rural people were disregarded. Even when projects for the disadvantaged were authorized, their funding and construction typically lagged far behind projects for the economically advantaged. For instance, the Navajo Indian Irrigation Project was neglected by the Bureau of Reclamation for over ten years until New Mexico senator Clinton Anderson eventually took the agency to task. When the Bureau of Reclamation finally built the dam, they tried to persuade the Navajos to accept less water than they believed they had been given by statute.[23] The conclusion of a number of authorities is that while the expertise and financial power of the federal government was harnessed to serve local elites in the West during the reclamation era, nothing like the same treatment was afforded to Indians during the development period.[24] Water users in Mexico were almost entirely ignored.

Although insiders characteristically shared information and opportunity to position themselves to secure economic advantage directly and indirectly, non-elites in localities often did not share in the benefits of projects. Heavy pressures for unity meant that details of allocation were left vague, and no real political discussion that might have mobilized the uninformed but affected took place.

Some of the unrepresented suffered severe negative consequences. Poor rural minorities found themselves slated for relocation because reservoirs were sited on their lands. Or they found themselves forced to sell their property and water rights because they could not afford to pay the higher taxes or water rates assessed for water development. The film and novel *The Milagro Beanfield War*, written by John Nichols, sympathetically explores this theme.

Change in the Pattern of Federal Water Development Politics

Even as the Colorado River Basin Act was authorized, basic revision in patterns of decision making was becoming clear. The incredible negotiation effort required to shepherd the legislation through Congress presaged difficulties to come. The change was felt most keenly in lack of effective support for approval and action on individual projects. The roots of the problem, however, were in systemic difficulties that had been highlighted shortly after World War II, problems that generated a major reform effort in the 1960s.

Federal water project development, which had reached a peak in the context of flood problems, regional economic development, and job creation in the 1930s, was sharply criticized by the two study commissions for government organization and efficiency chaired by former president Hoover in the late 1940s and mid-1950s. Opposition to expansion of public power generation was a factor, leading to private hydropower projects on the Snake, Deschutes, Clearwater, and other rivers in the 1950s and 1960s. Economic inefficiency, however, was the primary source of criticism.[25] Eisenhower (with the notable exception of the Upper Colorado River Storage Project Act of 1956) was a reluctant supporter of new federal projects. Project advocates in the Democratic Senate organized a select committee to formulate a rationale for reviving the project bandwagon.

The Water Resources Planning Act of 1965 (WRPA) was crafted to respond to Senate Select Committee recommendations. The WRPA was intended to provide an institutional structure for assessment of water problems and for water resources planning at national, regional, river basin, and project levels, and for selection and evaluation of specific projects. A companion bill authorized a nationwide water resources research program.

The WRPA was designed to provide a structural economic solution for legitimizing and diffusing opposition to projects. The act created a professionally staffed committee of secretaries and administrators of major water departments and agencies called the Water Resources Council. The council was to conduct the national and regional assessments of water problems, establish federal planning and evaluation procedures, guide and support river basin planning done by joint federal-state river basin planning groups, and administer a program of grants to strengthen state water planning.

WRPA was an ambitious effort to rationalize federal water development activities. The sponsorship of powerful congressional figures, endorsement by state government water officials, and a degree of involvement by cabinet officers and deputies in the Water Resources Council, had been thought to assure that the act would foster dependability and timeliness of congressional approval of well-considered federal projects. Instead, as one participant in the WRPA experience has written, the WRPA proved to be irrelevant.[26]

WRPA never became the focal point of the action in water politics. It erred in not providing an alternative to water projects as the preferred solution to water problems across the country. As long as the main matter to be decided was which states and districts were to be selected as sites for water projects, it was natural that local backers would appeal over the heads of WRPA planners to congressional representatives. President Carter poisoned congressional reception to the Water Resources Council by using it as an instrument of his "hit list" of water projects he wished to scuttle, and other unpopular regulations that tightened procedure for project evaluation. Because the elaborate assessment and planning procedures were largely irrelevant, the Water Resources Council and River Basin commissions lost visibility. The principal battles were fought in the arena of appropriations actions, omnibus water development bills, and a few major project controversies.

By 1985, the end of the water project development era was fixed. New starts in water resource development had become rarer. There was no true omnibus rivers and harbors legislation between 1970 and 1986. While the Water Resources Development Act of 1986 authorized a number of new projects, the budget presented by the president to Congress for fiscal year 1989–90 contained only five new starts for the Corps of Engineers and for the second year in a row none for the Bureau of Reclamation.[27] To some observers, however, pork barrel politics appeared to have life in it yet. In terms of budget expansion and contraction, the funding history of water resources agencies between 1951 and 1986 demonstrates marked ups and downs that are not much different from those of the domestic budget as a whole.[28] Yet Congress is spending its money differently, and in ways that do not bode well for satisfying water-related values through federal action. In 1984, for the first time the operations and management part of the budget for the Corps of Engineers exceeded construction and by the 1989 proposal, construction had fallen to 25 percent.

The decline in the number of new projects is due somewhat to physical realities. Good sites for new dams outside national parks and scenic areas have been all but used up. Political realities are far more telling. The costs of negotiating the congressional gauntlet to authorize projects have become higher and the benefits that local elites were likely to gain through federal projects have been lowered.

The growing power of the environmental movement at the national level introduced untenable conflict into the process of obtaining political approval of projects. Opposition by environmental groups cut into the unified local support prerequisite to a successful bid for project authorization. Congressional sponsors of proposed projects were forced to spend more time mediating conflict about the potentially environmentally damaging aspects of plans. Even when sponsors won congressional battles, it was not altogether certain that applause for bringing home the bacon would come from constituents. Detractors who could not be placated continued to maintain that water projects were environmental insults.

Further, legislators could no longer depend upon the mutual noninterference rules that once governed congressional water politics. Instead of respecting fellow legislators as the legitimate spokespersons of their districts' welfare, environmentally oriented and fiscally concerned members of Congress challenged whether water projects were anywhere in the public interest. In addition, legislators from eastern and midwestern districts expressed resentment that the distribution of pork through water projects was too skewed toward the West. All these forces lowered the rewards to congressional time and energy spent in water development advocacy.

Locally based political actors found better programs available through which to pursue pork barrel benefits. Federal water projects were much less attractive than the bonanza of wastewater treatment grants and smaller water supply programs, which operated through grants-in-aid. A gargantuan entrepreneurial effort such as that performed by Congressman Morris Udall in the Colorado River Basin Act was not required to steer construction grant projects through Congress.

Little by little Congress and the federal agencies became a less attractive forum in which local elites could pursue their water goals. Rules for evaluating federal water projects became increasingly stringent under the Water Resources Planning Act and as a result of criticisms of environmentalists and economists. Principles and standards of evaluation evolved to include not just national economic efficiency but also other "accounts," including environmental quality, social well-being, and regional economic development. In the Carter years evaluation criteria were given the force of regulations and environmental quality was elevated to equal importance with national economic efficiency. The National Environmental Policy Act of 1969 required the preparation of environmental impact statements, which introduced dangers of extended procedural delays and even cancellation of water projects.

As the federal agencies and Congress became less attractive arenas for water development interests, the access of environmental groups to these institutions improved. While these groups did not confront the ecological consequences of concentrated water management directly, some policy inroads were made on aspects of the water management issue, including wild and scenic rivers, endangered species, and riparian habitat. Desertification became the focus of agency reports and numerous federally sponsored conferences.

Beginning also in the Carter years, the notion that beneficiaries should bear most of the costs of water projects found its way into policy. Budget stringency sensitized the executive branch to the impact on budgets of big projects. The Carter reforms suggested that states pay 10 percent of project costs up front, and that private interests be required to pay back 25 percent over the life of projects. The idea that beneficiaries should pay was the cornerstone of the National Water Commission report in 1971 which, like Carter's Water Policy Task Force, turned out to be a little ahead of its time. By 1986 not only the president but also Congress had embraced the idea. The Water Resources Development Act enacted that year called for an equal financial contribution by nonfederal study sponsors during project planning, increased nonfederal cost shares for project construction, and up-front financing by locals of part of construction costs. After carefully reviewing the legislation, Cortner questioned whether locals would look upon federal programs as a boon or a burden.[29]

Development of a New Marketing Arena

In 1973, University of Arizona scholars Kelso, Martin, and Mack advised Arizonans that the answer to water scarcity lay not in the development of new supplies, but in the transfer of existing supplies to higher value uses.[30] The prescription was a familiar one often made by economists and, as they must have expected, it fell on deaf ears.[31] In the late 1980s, however, it has come to be conventional wisdom that water quantity problems be solved by conservation and reallocation. For instance, in 1985 Morris K. Udall spoke to a gathering of hydrogeologists. He said that Arizona's days of chasing new supplies when the old ones run out are over. "The emphasis is solidly on efficient use, wise management and conservation. We're turning away from exploring and developing new water sources."[32]

In 1980, Arizona enacted a groundwater reform act establishing the goal of safe yield for aquifers within Active Management Areas (AMAs) by the year 2025. An expanded state bureaucracy was to plan for gradual imposition of conservation requirements on all classes of user, with constraints on expansion of agriculture and incentives for reallocation of water from agriculture to municipal and industrial uses.[33] Under the terms of this legislation, Phoenix, Scottsdale, Tucson, and other municipalities have bought agricultural lands outside AMAs and intend to transfer water when needed. What is happening in terms of water transfers in Arizona is being repeated throughout the West, often on a larger scale.[34]

A number of factors are responsible for the emergence of the new marketing era. Some state officials were optimistic that state governments could take up some of the slack left by the winding down of federal construction programs, but state taxpayers were unenthusiastic about paying for water development funded at the state level. Especially during the period of the energy boom in the mid-1970s, the notion of go-it-alone water projects was actively considered. However, when faced with the reality of the bill for financing water development, state taxpayers have resisted strongly. In December of 1980, groups of disgruntled citizens gathered sufficient signatures to place a referendum on the ballot in California to approve or disapprove a group of facilities in the State Water Project, including the Peripheral Canal. Voters in the 1982 election that followed decisively defeated the expansion with huge majorities from northern California, the area of origin for water transfers. More significantly, strong opposition was also in evidence in southern California where taxpayers balked at the huge price tag involved.[35] Similar rejections were earlier dealt by voters to the Texas Water Plan.

Water users with expanding demands, particularly municipalities and energy companies, have been unwilling to accept the limits upon growth and the uncertainties that are placed by nature on the water supply in an arid land. Unless the energy companies could secure water rights of higher priority, they were vulnerable to the frequent droughts characteristic of lands west of the 100th meridian. In the 1970s energy projects, including the coal-fired Intermountain Power Project in Utah and the Sun Desert nuclear power plant in southern Utah, began buying water rights in anticipation of the energy boom. While some of these projects have been scaled back, they set the stage for later rural-to-urban water transfers.

Exploding cities all around the West, including Phoenix, Tucson, Denver, Albuquerque, Santa Fe, El Paso, and San Diego, grew at approximately three times the national urban average in the 1970 to 1980 decade. Most had already pursued all cheap water supply options in their immediate vicinity. Cities within the Active Management Areas defined by the Arizona Groundwater Management Act were especially constrained since they needed to show a secure 100-year supply to support new developments. Every Sun Belt city sees itself becoming Los Angeles—of course without the problems—if physical constraint of water availability can be overcome.

Under traditional water law, the position of newcomers, or junior rights holders, is quite weak. As participants in the market, however, municipalities and industries have a strong hand. Water is an essential but low-cost component for producing energy, and utilities and other energy producers can afford to pay a high price. Most municipal water rates have been artificially low as utilities have charged the average rather than the marginal price for water and modest rate increases have small effects on water use. Further, new supplies can be funded by bonds or taxes. There is flexibility for municipal water companies to raise capital to become buyers in water markets.

Family farmers and agriculturally based rural areas have lost ground politically and economically. Many of the highest priority water rights are held by agriculture and 85 percent of water in most western states has gone to farming. In terms of water deliveries, agriculture was the major beneficiary of federal water development. The intention of reclamation was originally to further the family farm and to bring more land under cultivation. As water programs in concert with other federal agriculture programs have worked out in practice, a concentration of land ownership has resulted. In California, the tendency toward concentration was heightened with the development of the State Water Project. The state's subsidized system of pricing and entitlements helped launch a major buying spree in the Kern County area in the late 1960s and early 1970s. Multinational corporations such as Tenneco, Prudential Life Insurance, Shell Oil, and Standard Oil of California took over huge tracts of land, much of it previously marginal to farming. Cheap water made possible specialty crop development.

The economics of farming has now changed. Most of the family farmers have been pushed out. Corporations are quite willing to sell water and land, especially if they can reap windfall profits from federal water developments subsidized under the original guise of egalitarian social purposes. Contemporary agribusiness has much more influence in the market than in politics. At the same time, a poor agricultural economy and changing demographics have left rural agriculturalists and family farmers in a poor position to act politically to protect their grip on water.

Reliance on marketing of water rights to determine water distributions satisfies water policy critics who wish for greater efficiency in allocation. Federal water development projects were vulnerable to the charge of being poor investments. In contrast, water reallocation could be rationalized as leading to greater efficiency. Even environmentalists were impressed by this argument when it was realized that reallocation was an alternative to dams. Certain so-called efficiency measures could stretch existing supplies and were much more cost effective than big capital development projects. The Berkeley office of the Environmental Defense Fund became one of the foremost advocates of the economic approach. A proposal whereby water conservation works in the Imperial Irrigation District could be funded by the metropolitan water department in exchange for the salvaged water was strongly put forward by these environmentalists.

The judiciary has reinforced the approval of the marketplace as an appropriate arena for water allocation. In *Sporhase v. Nebraska* in 1982, the United States Supreme Court declared that water was a commodity subject to interstate commerce clause scrutiny and that public ownership of water asserted by most western state statutes and constitutions was a legal fiction.[36] There can be little doubt that the attitude of the court provided a strong impetus for rural-to-urban water transfers. The Sporhase case set an important precedent for the city of El Paso's attempt to secure water rights in the lower Rio Grande in New Mexico, arguing that the efforts of the agriculturalists in the area to protect their water and rural lifestyle was economic protectionism.

The transaction or decision-making costs in water transfers are low relative to the political water development process. Instead of the byzantine process of building support for federal water resources development described in this book and made even more torturous later by elaboration of regulations, market exchanges required only a willing buyer and seller and a showing of nonimpairment of protected interests. Courts defend third-party interests in water transfers, but nothing like the full range of protections for the environment and broader social goals that operated in federal water development. Expansion of new or augmented water uses can take place throughout the market without going through an environmental impact statement or the test of value preferences that consent building for legislation involved. The mechanism of water marketing skirts the threat of federal reserved water rights, particularly as they apply to Indian tribes. If marketing can be extended sufficiently, it is conceivable that tribal rights could be bought out. In any case, the shutdown in the pipeline of federal money for projects has meant that tribes will have little public money to develop their water if they choose not to sell.

Transfers are not without opposition, and a number of political and legal roadblocks have kept the exchange of water through markets to a rather modest pace. Objections have been raised in Congress to allowing farmers to reap profits from selling water developed at subsidized costs for reclamation purposes. Even in those cases where Indian tribes are in favor of the lease or sale of water for off-reservation use, waivers to the Non-Intercourse Act are considerably difficult to obtain. State legislatures have debated and sometimes adopted laws regulating the rural-to-urban transfer of water. Some agricultural entities, like the Elephant Butte Irrigation District, have used their political and legal power to delay and undermine water transfers. Despite these impediments, however, few doubt that markets are to become the future forum for water exchange.

Winners and Losers in Contemporary Politics of Water

The apologists for water marketing typically argue that the losers are either nonexistent or few, and that they generally deserve their fate. Market discipline has a therapeutic effect. When markets work properly, there is a willing buyer and a willing seller, and the supposed result is that both are better off. Presumably potential sellers are free to simply refuse to sell and avoid any perceived losses. Society also benefits by the transaction since resources are reallocated to the higher value use. The shift away from the federal purse eliminates the free riders or rent seekers who gain benefits without paying, as well as the wasteful bureaucracy serving narrow clientele. The most salient characteristic of the political perceptions about the distributive pattern of politics prevailing during the development era, which is the focus of this book, was that there were only winners and no losers. Yet, as Lowi points out, all policies are redistributive in the long run, helping some at the expense of others.[37] And, as discussed above, this was the case in the era of big federal projects. Similarly, contemporary market-oriented patterns of politics favor some interests over others. At the beginning of the chapter certain constants of water politics were identified. These constants at work through contemporary water institutions produce definite winners and losers.

Winners

1. Growth and development interests continue to get water they desire for security and opportunity. The predominant growth and development interests today are urban areas, which are aggressively acquiring water rights. As De Young and Jenkins-Smith point out, the classic model of markets has little to do with the exchanges taking place.[38] Instead of an individual buyer and independent seller, purchases are likely to be made by collective entities such as municipal water utilities that are spending the ratepayers' and taxpayers' money. When sellers are independent farmers, they do not participate on an equal footing with municipal water utilities because of their relative lack of economic power.

   Of course some farmers are able to sell their water rights to support low-profit agriculture or "grow margaritas" in retirement communities. There may also be some water entrepreneurs who are able to make considerable profits buying and selling water. In 1984 a group of private investors who had senior water rights in Meeker, Colorado, sold an option to lease between 300,000 and 500,00 acre-feet per year of water to San Diego for $10,000. While this particular lease was not consummated, others like it are being widely discussed. In 1987 a realtor in Arizona was advertising property for what was claimed to be one-third of what could be earned through water sales.[39]

   A primary aim of the funding reforms for federal water projects was to force beneficiaries to pay more. Theoretically, urban expansion of water supply systems are paid for by customers. In actuality, however, costs have been externalized through a variety of mechanisms. Urban water system development expenses are spread over all users rather than being concentrated to affect mainly those who profit from expansion. Bond issues have long pay-back periods so that future residents share in costs.
2. Federal taxpayers have enjoyed lower water development costs. The treasury of the nation is no longer drained into localities that are the main beneficiaries of water development projects. In this sense, the federal taxpayer is no longer among the losers as was the case during the water development era. At the same time, certain social purposes for which the federal taxpayer once invested money have now been moved off the agenda. The agrarian dream that drove the adoption of the Newlands Act, which intended to make lands available in the West to the common people, failed then faded.

Losers

1. Environmentalists would not be classified among the losers if evaluation were to be made on the basis of victories in political battles over

water resources policy. Today, fewer development projects threaten to destroy natural areas, and some environmentalists perceive the taming of the federal construction program as sufficient accomplishment to compensate for whatever sacrifices now may be involved in contemporary water decisions. Citing examples like the modifications of the CAP and Animas–La Plata, as described in chapter 9, one environmentalist noted that the movement had succeeded in sanding off many of the rough edges of projects that were admittedly still flawed in concept. Better projects are now being designed, this environmentalist argued, including ones which consider nonstructural alternatives because cost-sharing reforms have forced local decision makers to look for less expensive ways of meeting water goals.[40] As the history of the Water Resources Development Act makes clear, water legislation must obtain the blessing of environmentalists if it is to be passed by Congress. New projects will contain features mitigating adverse impacts to environmental values. Water conservation, in the sense of cutting back on water use, has gained increased attention.

Environmentalist gains must be weighed against significant losses that are as yet not well recognized by spokespersons for the movement. The institutional mechanisms for managing water effectively are deteriorating.[41] States and localities lack the jurisdiction or interest to adopt systemic or river basin perspectives on water management. Municipal water managers place a higher priority upon assured water supply than upon the social and ecological dislocations that may result from their market transactions. Because water rights or their priority are moved rather than wet water, it is often difficult to evaluate and mobilize to protect against adverse impacts of transfers. The natural limit which aridity imposes upon ecology is disregarded by human residents in the West as much as or more than in the past.

Further, environmentalists have lost an important handle on growth in arid regions. A vast reservoir of water previously used by agriculture is now available. Lack of water is therefore not a good argument for defeating energy development projects. Water shortage does not provide a credible argument to limit population expansion in most western cities as access to new supplies is gained through the water markets. Moving water from farms and rural areas has become legitimate even though the resulting use of water is much more environmentally damaging. To substitute housing developments with attendant problems of cars and air pollution, garbage disposal, and water pollution for cotton fields with fertilizers, pesticides, and water pollution, may not be such an excellent environmental bargain. Large populations in arid regions may have less flexibility in adjusting to the inevitable periodic droughts or to the long-term climate change that some scientists predict. Adverse environmental impacts also take place in areas of origin in water transfers. Retired farmland, especially if it has been laser leveled, only very slowly recovers natural vegetation. Blowing dust and tumbleweeds on fallow lands in the Avra Valley area in Arizona, bought by the city of Tucson for water rights, are illustrative.

Environmentalists have limited access to the market forums where water reallocation decisions occur. Environmental groups succeeded in putting in place procedural protections that would insure that environmental values be taken into account in federal water policy, but now this machinery affords little protection. Third-party and more general social interests are poorly represented by buyers and sellers in market transactions. States have begun to institute public welfare criteria allowing government to intervene in sales, leases, and transfers when broad social interests are at stake, but this legislative activity is in the early stages.[42]

2. Disadvantaged people including Indians and other rural minorities continue to lose in water decisions. Without question the extent of participation of disadvantaged people in water politics has grown.[43] Instead of being left out of negotiations on water projects, the supposed benefits to Indian people and tribal support have rescued several projects from near certain defeat as the Central Arizona and Animas–La Plata projects experience illustrates. There is a difference, however, between gaining a place at the bargaining table and being able to control the substance or direction of the bargains being struck. Disadvantaged people have won something through a number of contemporary water developments, but that something is often quite remote from what they really wanted. Moreover, just as they were beginning to succeed, the water game changed. After dedicating many of their brightest young members to training in the law and winning greater security of water rights through the courts, the federal construction program began winding down. Poor people no longer have much opportunity to develop their water resources with federal help. What construction money is available is overlaid with financing and evaluation requirements much stricter than those applied to development projects in the past.

Poor rural people are unlikely to profit from water sales because much of their attachment to the resource is noneconomic.[44] Loss of water represents a sacrifice of opportunity, security, and self-determination. Research indicates that the predominant opinion in many rural communities is against sales, leases, and transfers of water.[45] Rural respondents reflect a conviction that while a few individuals may be willing to sell and may profit thereby, the community as a whole will be worse off.

3. Federal construction agencies have doubtless lost ground in the current pattern of politics. The author of a most critical book published in the 1950s on the Army Corps of Engineers observes the present corps as a pale image of its former self.[46] Power began to be shifted away from the

agency with the establishment of the position of assistant secretary of the army for civil works in 1970 and has continued since.[47]

The Bureau of Reclamation has been even more devastated. A reorganization of the bureau considered in 1987 would have at first moved the commissioner from the centers of power in Washington to Denver, an unlikely proposal in the 1960s era of Floyd Dominy.[48]

To some extent state and local water agencies have benefited from the diminution of federal authority. Water policy making is a good deal more decentralized than previously. This shift has had its price, however. Some state agencies are weak and lack the means to manage water resources effectively, especially when this entails regulating powerful local interests. State interests often conflict when it comes to management of river basins which cross state lines.

Lessons To Be Learned

"The more things change, the more they remain the same" was first said in French, and not about the politics of water.[49] Yet the somewhat discouraging insight aptly sums up the analysis presented in this chapter. Measured against the standard of politics of the Colorado River basin legislation of 1968, there have been profound changes in many aspects of water politics. Yet the constants set forth at the beginning of the chapter remain virtually unaltered.

The product or output of water policy is vastly different from twenty years ago when results were counted in terms of new projects in the water development pipeline. Today success in water politics is measured in paper rather than concrete. Water rights sales and lease agreements have replaced bulldozers.

The forums for decision making have shifted radically. Congress was the arena in which water policy was made in the 1960s. In the late 1960s and 1970s, federal forums were restructured and opened to environmental and other social influences. Through grants-in-aid and other devices, power was increasingly shifted to the state and local levels. Finally in the 1980s, decision-making authority was reallocated to large private or quasi-public agencies including public utilities as water markets became a preferred method of augmenting supplies.

Alterations in forums have had a clear impact upon the openness of access to decision making. In the era of the Colorado River Basin Act, key participants manipulated the system to exclude and discredit interests that could not be accommodated and brought into the consensus. Even so, when something as essential to their core interest as the Grand Canyon was at stake, environmentalists were able to force their way into the congressional arena. Their purview of influence, however, was narrow, usually affecting only the margins of water policy. Numbers of changes in evaluation procedures, environmental laws, and congressional incentives

23

in the 1970s opened the federal decision-making process in water to include previously excluded interests.

Participation at the state level and in the market forums to which decision-making activities have shifted in the 1980s appears to again be confined to a relatively small circle of interests. No authoritative study of present-day state water agencies exists upon which to base conclusions about participation. In Arizona, however, environmentalists told interviewers that while they had some influence over water quality decisions, they had relatively little say in allocation decisions.[50] It might be theorized that the direct interest of local taxpayers in decisions related to the allocation of money to be used either to share costs of projects or to buy or lease water rights would prompt both greater controversy and public involvement. However, the financing of water policy is a complex, uncertain issue requiring specialized interest and skills. It is not the kind of issue around which the public easily mobilizes unless it is accompanied by other more volatile matters such as the northern versus southern California split on the Peripheral Canal.

The outcome of water policy in terms of winners and losers has changed only slightly in the past twenty years. Development-oriented local elites were the main beneficiaries of the federal water development era. These interests continue to be the winners in prevailing patterns of water decisions. The previous losers, especially environmentalists, Indians, and poor rural people, while more influential than previously, continue to lose. For environmentalists there are some positive tradeoffs involved in the demise of big federal projects, but environmentally damaging water decisions continue. Indians have gained a place at the bargaining table, but the prizes they win are sometimes far from what they really want. Other interests that used to do better now fare poorly, including rural economies dependent on irrigated agriculture, and federal construction agencies. Further, the likelihood that a fundamental reshuffling of winners and losers will take place appears increasingly remote. With little unappropriated water remaining in the West, with groundwater levels falling in a large number of river basins, and with ground- and surface water quality experiencing degradation, little flexibility remains to serve previously neglected interests without encountering entrenched opposition.

The lessons to be gained from this overview of water policy for policy analysts are sobering. It may well be that policy design—that is, the content of laws, and the process of decision making including the identification of forums and decision rules—matter much less to outcomes than policy analysts suppose. The capacity of dominant interests to pursue advantages despite changes in decision making appears to be large. The overriding forces in water policy may be the nature and perceptions of the issue, and the political influence, resources, and skill of the local growth-oriented interests. The overexploitation of water resources continues to take place whether it is facilitated through construction projects or the marketing of water rights to users remote from the areas in which water naturally occurs. Until aridity is accepted as a natural limit to which humans must adapt their expectations and institutions, water resource decisions will continue to pay insufficient attention to impacts on the environment and the social and cultural values associated with this fundamental resource.

2

The 1968 Case Study Introduced

The Nature of the Problem

The press and Arizona political leaders celebrated September 30, 1968, the date President Johnson signed the Colorado River Basin Act, as the greatest day for Arizona since statehood. After over twenty years of struggle for congressional approval, the Central Arizona Project, designed to carry water from the mainstream of the Colorado River through a series of aqueducts to the Phoenix and Tucson areas, was at last authorized. Less prominently, many New Mexicans took satisfaction from the passage of the Colorado River Basin Act. For tucked within the act of Congress were two water development projects affecting New Mexico. Why and how New Mexico has achieved this share of Arizona's victory is the central concern here.

The two New Mexico projects were physically unrelated, being located in the northwest and southwest corners of the state. One project was intended to substantially put to use the remainder of New Mexico's entitlement to upper Colorado River basin water under the 1948 compact between Colorado, New Mexico, Utah, and Wyoming. The other project adds 18,000 acre-feet of water available to New Mexico on the Gila, a tributary that flows through New Mexico and Arizona to the Colorado River. The two projects can be briefly described as follows.

The Animas–La Plata Project in southwestern Colorado and northwestern New Mexico was essentially an irrigation project, although it also promised some municipal and industrial benefits. The Animas and La Plata rivers originate in Colorado and flow southward in parallel courses to the San Juan River in New Mexico. The Animas River has the larger and higher drainage area and the larger flow. The area of irrigable land in the Animas River basin is limited and had already been developed as far as is practical. The larger land area in the La Plata River basin was in need of a greater and more dependable water supply. And the newly authorized project promised just such a supply, for it consisted of storing and regulating the Animas River and diverting its flow into the La Plata River basin.

Hooker Dam or a suitable alternative in southwestern New Mexico, also authorized by the Colorado River Basin Act, was a water storage project on the Gila River. The project was intended to allow New Mexico to increase its present uses by 18,000 acre-feet per year and would provide flood control, recreation, irrigation, municipal and industrial storage, and other benefits. Downstream users of the Gila in Arizona would lose water as a result of Hooker Dam. To make up this loss, water exchanges with central Arizona were anticipated.

On its face, the inclusion of these two projects in a bill authorizing the Central Arizona Project was a curious event. The connection between the projects in New Mexico and Arizona was neither direct nor clear, and insofar as the effects of these two projects upon the CAP could be traced, they were detrimental. In terms of hydrology and engineering, economics and financing, the association of these projects in a single package appeared irrational; its rationale appears only when the politics of the Colorado River Basin Act are laid out.

Project Factors

The site of the Animas–La Plata Project is remote from the location of the Arizona waterworks. The building of this upper basin project is in no way necessary to the building and operation of the CAP. In fact, more water would be available to central Arizona from the Colorado River if the Animas–La Plata Project were postponed, or not built at all. Its concurrent consideration and construction was not necessarily prescribed by considerations of long-range planning. The Pacific Southwest Water Plan, drawn up by the Department of the Interior and presented in 1964, was an ambitious attempt at comprehensive regional planning of water development.[1] Besides the CAP, the plan contained recommendations for features of various sorts in Nevada, California, and New Mexico, but no upper basin project was recommended or even considered.

On the other hand, proposals for the Central Arizona Project, including the Pacific Southwest Water Plan, regularly included Hooker Dam. For the CAP itself, however, Hooker was quite expendable. In fact, as in the case of the upper basin project, more water would be available to central Arizona if the dam were to be eliminated. The relationship here operates in the reverse: The CAP was a physical prerequisite for Hooker. Without the construction of the Central Arizona Project, the additional water necessary for exchange to satisfy the Gila users in Arizona would not be available. New Mexico, then, could not increase its uses on the Gila through storage at the Hooker project without jeopardizing present uses in Arizona.

Beyond physical considerations, the association of the two New Mexico projects with the Central Arizona Project in the Colorado River Basin Act cannot be explained in terms of economic feasibility. The direct benefit/cost ratio of the Animas–La Plata Project was a fairly low 1.1 to 1. The cost per acre and the investment per farm were quite high.[2] Consequently, its addition to the Colorado River Basin Act did nothing to improve the package economically. Instead, it operated to reduce the benefit/cost ratio of the CAP since it used water that otherwise would be employed to increase the benefits of the Arizona project.

The economic relationship of Hooker Dam to the CAP was (as in the case of its physical connection) one of dependency, with all the benefits of the association accruing to New Mexico. Standing by itself, Hooker was not an economically practicable project.[3] Were the usual benefit/cost standards applied to the project, there was no likelihood that the ratio would be unity or better. The project had therefore to be embraced as a part of the CAP in order to be in any way economically justifiable. Yet obviously the addition of an uneconomic project to the package did not improve its overall economics. The financial underpinnings of the New Mexico projects were another matter to be considered.

Financially, the ties of the Animas–La Plata Project were to the Upper Basin Development Fund which was distinct from the repayment arrangements made for the CAP. The project was heavily subsidized by power revenues accumulated from dams in the upper basin above Lees Ferry. Quite separately, a special fund was created in the Colorado River Basin Act, its monies being derived partly from power revenues at Hoover, Parker, and Davis dams attributable to Arizona to finance the CAP. Financially, then, this northwestern New Mexico–southwestern Colorado project was distinctly independent of the CAP while Hooker was financially dependent upon it. In fact, the latter is something of a financial liability. Since Hooker Dam could not pay for itself, it would have to rely on the CAP's development fund. Clearly Hooker would be more a burden than an aid to the pay out of the CAP.

Since physical, economic, and financial considerations do not adequately explain the inclusion of the two New Mexico projects in the Colorado River Basin Act, it is possible that they were simply added because they were ready for consideration by Congress. But an examination of the state of planning and a review of the projects at the moment of their injection into the bill indicate that the addition of these projects was not a coincidence of timing. A feasibility report had been completed by the Bureau of Reclamation on the Animas–La Plata Project early in 1962. This report, however, had not been cleared by the Bureau of the Budget by the spring of 1966 when the inclusion of the project and four others in Colorado became live issues. During that spring the project was hurriedly revised to meet more adequately the Budget Bureau standards, and the project was rushed through review. Budget acted on the project in less than a month, nearly a record-setting pace.

Studies of only a little better than reconnaissance level had been completed on Hooker Dam when it was presented before Congress for authorization along with the CAP. The design characteristics of Hooker Dam were adopted from earlier studies made by the Army Corps of Engineers on flood control, and had first been presented by the Bureau of Reclamation in 1947. Cost levels had been updated to 1963, but the features of the plan had not been worked out in any detail.[4] Thorough study of Hooker or suitable alternatives was thus left until after authorization. Therefore, in the case of Hooker Dam as well as Animas–La Plata, timing and planning were made to accommodate congressional consideration of the Colorado River Basin Act.

It is possible to speculate that the needs for these two projects in New Mexico were so imperative as to justify their inclusion in any available vehicle leading toward immediate authorization. Yet here, too, a look at the expected benefits lends little support to the notion that the needs were of sudden or crisis proportions. The desire for additional irrigation water in the La Plata basin was long standing. Although the Animas–La Plata had received designation for priority planning in the Colorado River Storage Project Act of 1956, work on the project had continued in a routine fashion until 1966. Nor were the municipal and industrial uses added to the project in its revision in response to critical demand. Indeed, the Bureau of the Budget noted in its review of the project that there appeared to be no immediate need for the municipal and industrial water to be delivered to the Ute Mountain Reservation for the development of a coal-steam power plant, although the inclusion of these uses improved the economics of the project.[5] And, in fact, the bureau questioned the desirability of the project as a whole without further consideration of all the alternative uses for water. This, of course, implied approval of at least a postponement in authorization.

The need for Hooker Dam is indicated by an assessment of the benefits. A reservoir at the Hooker site was supposed to provide water for consumptive use in New Mexico as follows:

Municipal and industrial	10,800 acre-feet
Agriculture	700 acre-feet
Reservoir evaporation	6,400 acre-feet

Most of the municipal and industrial water was supposed to go to mining and milling operations. The only concrete source of future demand was the Phelps-Dodge Corporation then contemplated for Tyrone, New Mexico, and water rights on the Gila and tributaries had already been acquired by the company sufficient to fill this potential demand. Use of the new municipal and industrial water would then fall to the other mining and milling companies, possibly seven, which were then exploring or operating in the Gila River basin in New Mexico.[6] None of these companies had firm plans for use of the water at the time Hooker Dam was authorized, and nearby water is not a primary determinant for opening a mine or a mill. Demand for water from the Hooker project, then, was not immediate, but something anticipated for the future.

The Key to Understanding

The only remaining explanation for the addition of the New Mexico projects to the Colorado River Basin Act was obviously politics since neither the imperatives of engineering or economics nor the logic of events provided justification. The rationale of politics is separate and often quite different from the justifications supplied by other professions. Political feasibility is an exercise of intuition and insight, a "seat of the pants" judgment made by the political actors most involved and experienced in making policy decisions.[7] And from the point of view of the political actors involved in the passage of the Colorado River Basin Act, the addition of Animas–La Plata and Hooker Dam was justified on the basis of political feasibility.

To comprehend the combination of projects in the Colorado River Basin Act, it is therefore necessary to see water projects from the political actor's perspective. The political actors involved in influencing public policy cannot simply make judgments. They must build support for their decisions. They must exercise continual foresight. They must take care not only of their ability to influence but also of the consequences of actions and events upon their future ability to influence. The political feasibility of the New Mexico projects entailed the judgment of the actors shaping the Colorado River Basin Act that the balance of support over opposition generated by these projects was positive.

It is assumed here that the political calculations made on the New Mexico projects were cases in a general pattern. Making policy in any field, including water development, is an ongoing affair. The projects in the Colorado River Basin Act were part of a continuous stream of water proposals treated by the policy-making process. The political institutions involved in the process have a degree of stability. Therefore, although some calculations of political feasibility are peculiar to individual political actors in particular circumstances, the sources of support existing for decisions in the field tend to remain constant. The nature of this support can be explored; its origins can be traced to certain fundamental perceptions about who is likely to be hurt and who is likely to be helped by decisions. The manner in which this support can expand and be capitalized upon can be plotted. The result is a kind of abstract pattern or model of political feasibility in a field.

The initial objective of this study is to develop such a model, a model of the political process in water development decisions. It will indicate in a general way the criteria that proposals must satisfy to be politically feasible. The secondary objective is to test the relevance of this model in the case of New Mexico's role in the Colorado River Basin Act. If the model is successful, it will explain far better than engineering, economics, or events how New Mexico got its share in this piece of legislation.

3

A Model of Political Feasibility in Water Development Policy

Introduction

Public policies determine who gets the what, when, and how of the goods and services at the command of the government. Every public policy helps some and not others and, at times, aids some to the detriment of others. Different policies cut across the various interests of the public in a multitude of ways. Some policies offer benefits to a number of discrete interests without posing any direct threats. Some offer indulgences to certain groups while imposing deprivations upon others. And still other policies may favor a whole social class at the expense of another stratum of society.[1]

The fundamental assumption here is that the various kinds of issues have characteristic patterns of politics. The risks and rewards perceived as resulting from policy choices are the basic variables that affect the decision-making structure. The benefits and costs anticipated provoke, demand, and provide inducements for particular political actors to involve themselves in the policy-making process. Once certain political actors are energized by an issue, the particular political arenas in which decisions are made are marked out since the involved actors, or activists, will gravitate toward settings where they have access and where the distribution of power resources maximizes their impact. The stakes in the issue and the kinds of actors engaged in policy making affect the way actors relate to one another in building support and in dealing with opposition to policy. Finally, the nature of the issue, the consequent actors involved, the relevant arenas, and the characteristic relationships among actors are all related to the sort of policy which is made and to whether a change in policy is incremental or innovative.

The task of this chapter is to examine the nature of water development as a political issue. It will be necessary to know who stands to gain from the policy-making process in water development and to know who is likely to feel threatened and how. Once these basic forces in the pattern of politics have been identified, the other parts of the decision-making structure— the actors, the political arenas, and the consent-building relationships—

can be traced to complete the pattern.

The Issue[2]

The key attribute of water as a political issue is its basis in a locality. Both the need for water development and the possible benefit from water projects are perceived in local terms. This is largely a result of the nature of water resources. Water, like land, has a geographic location. Its supply and quality vary tremendously from place to place. Consequently, water problems are seen as local problems. People in areas where water is in short supply feel they have little in common with localities experiencing pollution. Even areas with common problems of scarcity seldom perceive shared interests. Rather, localities in the same river basin or in adjacent basins where diversion is possible fiercely compete for water supply and development funds.

The physical character of water projects further contributes to notions of localized stakes, for water projects are geographically situated in a limited area, with few extending over more than a congressional district or over, at most, a state. Whatever the benefit/cost ratio to the nation which an economist may establish for a project, the benefits are heaped upon the small portion of the nation where the project is located. The local economy gets the initial impetus from construction activity. Other benefits, including recreation, irrigation, flood control, and even power, also tend to be greatest in the immediate project area.

In addition to such physical considerations, water, as an issue, has a certain emotional message which appeals powerfully to local sentiment. Water is seen as wealth: A boom is bound to occur if an area has water and can develop it. A locality sees benefits in water beyond any specific uses; water carries a guarantee of a prosperous future. Even when it would seem that an area has more water than it could possibly put to use, local people are loath to part with or even to share its riches. Belief in the ability of water to create prosperity is so strong that, at times, even a preliminary study of a water project can create a local boom. Merchants increase their stock, and land values go up. Strong local pressure then exists to go on and build the project.[3]

Wherever water is situated, it is locally thought of as "our" water. Landowners' tendency to claim all the water on their premises has created special problems in the arid West where upstream development can leave downstream users high and dry. A complex system of western water law has grown up to cope with this difficulty, but rather than abolishing the proprietary notion of water, the law reinforces it. The rule of prior appropriation states that the first place where water is put to beneficial use has established a priority over all other areas and over alternate water uses which come later in time. The holder of the senior right possesses the water. Though the right is granted for a specific place, in most states it can be moved with consent of joint interests, but transferring to a new locale is difficult. Legislation, compacts, and agreements have modified the doctrine of "first in time, first in right," but they have not affected the water ownership belief. As a rule, they only reshuffle entitlements without challenging the idea that localities have a title to their water.

Historically, the experience of localities in water development issues has supported the Midas-touch notion about water and the appropriateness of the provincial viewpoint on water issues. Water development has in the past very often been the key to growth. It has certainly been so in southern California and, to a lesser extent, in the Northwest. Once an area has developed its water, it has acted to protect its development with political muscle commensurate with its increased wealth. The object lesson to other states is the necessity of self-interest and self-protection. If the locality does not or cannot pursue its own projects, its interests and rights are bound to be ignored.

In any policy-making pattern, the form in which policy problems arise affects the perceptions of stakes in the particular issue and the way the issue is worked on in the policy process.[4] In water, the policy-making process is ignited by a specific project proposal pushed by locally oriented persons or groups with sufficient influence to stimulate public discussion. Typically, some local businessman, or water user, or locally based bureaucrat in a water agency, or group composed of these people, supplies the basic drive for water development. However diverse the desires of initiators may be—water supply, economic growth, recreation, an expanded role for some agency, etc.—they all perceive a stake in having some specific project constructed.

The focus of the policy-making process from the very beginning is on a specific project, shortcutting both a general discussion of goals and a consideration of alternative means of achieving chosen goals. This discourages broad national involvement. The narrow form in which the issue is posed fails to stimulate consideration of the value of achieving some aim which has been identified vis-à-vis other goals. The issue is not presented as a demand for clean water, plentiful water, or expansion of the economy in a particular region through water development. Were the issue so presented, the worth of these goals might then be balanced against other demands such as adequate housing and space travel in a political process in which a wide range of interests would perceive a stake.

Project proposals with a fair amount of detail are readily available for locally oriented interests to attach themselves to, especially in the West. Various water agencies for decades have been identifying possible dam sites and studying various waterworks which might be built. The primary benefits expected from a project proposal may change substantially from the time of initial studies until the time of active consideration. A flood-control project may ultimately emerge as a facility for recreation. The main lines of the project plan, however, usually remain set over the years. This is partly due to the attachment which localities have to specific proposals which have aroused their expectations, and partly because of the tremendous lead time which project planning requires.

The Activists

Which persons and groups become the activists, the prime movers in the pattern of policy making, is directly related to how stakes in an issue are perceived. In making the decision to invest time, energy, and resources to affect the direction of decisions in a policy area, potential activists must consider the nature and significance of support they will derive from their activity. Some activists have no choice but involvement with particular issues because so many of the demands which the activists must satisfy to maintain their influence and position dictate accordingly. Other activists have considerable leeway in determining their involvement. Still others can look for erosion of their support if they become engaged in policy making on a given issue.

Consequently a range of different levels of involvement exists. The more relevant the issue is to the activist, the more likely it will be that the activist will engage in the initiation and formulation of policy. When the issue area is of less immediate concern, the activist will confine efforts to building support for and legitimizing various policy decisions. The sort of involvement which an activist settles upon depends, at least in some measure, upon personal judgment of efficacy. All else being equal, political actors concentrate on issues where they can expect to have some impact on the policy outcome. This means they make an overall assessment of the pattern of policy making in an area, and of how they might relate to other participants in it.[5]

Since the basis for water as an issue is in the locality, persons and groups which are locally oriented and sensitive to local pressures are the activists in water development. It has already been noted that the genesis of water proposals is in the locality. Local interests provide the initiating energy for water development.[6] Government agencies on the state and local level are oriented toward localities.

State water agencies, moreover, play a significant role in selecting which project proposals are put on the active agenda for federal authorization, and these agencies are sensitive to local sentiment. Their organizational frameworks frequently represent different sections of the state. Federal government agencies which participate in formulating project proposals and have the assignment of building and operating projects are responsive to the local drive which is basic to water policy making. According to Arthur Maass, one of the first steps which the Army Corps of Engineers takes in a preliminary examination of a project proposal is to hold a public hearing during which the corps is informed about the desires of various persons and groups, the interests which would benefit, and the local cooperation that may be expected.[7] Concern with localities is just as obvious in the project planning done by the Bureau of Reclamation. It is also reflected in the personnel and structure of the agency. Bureau officials are often native to the seventeen western states in which the bureau operates.[8] Bureau personnel are reputed to be "homesteaders" with a tendency to stay in one place for long periods of time, becoming part of the community and sharing in local interests. The national headquarters of the Bureau of Reclamation was located in Denver until the 1940s, and the engineering and hydrology sections are still centered there.

The political environment of many congressmen favors activism on water issues. Congressmen, particularly House members, are tied closely to localities. The areas they represent are relatively small and homogeneous, and any forceful grassroots movement behind a water project is dangerous for the member of Congress to ignore. Members of Congress themselves are recruited in such a way as to orient them toward the locality. Lifetime or long-term residents of the state or congressional district are favored in the electoral process.[9] Further, many members of Congress see their role as locals who read local newspapers, recruit their staff from the home district, and look at issues in terms of local impact.[10] Such members of Congress see their job as furthering the interests of their constituency, including pushing along water projects which the local people believe will benefit them.

In contrast, the president, persons and groups within the institution of the presidency, and top executives within the administration face little which compels involvement in water issues. Indeed, exerting time and energy on such matters is a risky undertaking. The president has a nationwide constituency and must be wary of local controversies which add little to his support and threaten to sap his power resources. He has many demands on his attention, and his responsibilities are greater than his power. He must be frugal in investing his influence.[11] Consequently he usually remains aloof from water politics.

The Office of Management and Budget (OMB) has only a tentative stake in affecting decisions on water projects. As a staff arm of the presidency, its support comes mainly from the chief executive and, as a result, it shares some of his perceptions of the risks of involvement in water policy. It also partakes of the urban, social welfare biases of the presidency, which puts water projects for irrigation and reclamation on low priority. Economists in the OMB believe in economic feasibility as a test for water projects. Low benefit/cost ratios render projects unjustifiable in the eyes of the OMB, and it feels some stake in preventing authorization of such projects. However, given the lack of immediate interest and proximate position to the formulation of proposals, the OMB frequently does not exert itself on projects it might wish to oppose.

The secretary of the interior shares some of the president's problems. Attempts to exercise strong leadership on the secretary's part usually arouse criticism from local representatives whose locality fails to get the secretary's endorsement for projects. If these discontented local representatives have much influence in Congress, the secretary's opinions will probably not carry much weight in ultimate policy. Further, strong initiatives by the secretary of the interior in water development are likely to provoke an intradepartmental controversy between the secretary and the locally supported Bureau of Reclamation and other Interior agencies with different orientations, but also concerned with water development. The secretary may minimize risk by standing aloof from the initiation and formulation of proposals and by withholding involvement until localities and agencies have worked out their differences.

The Political Arena

The real testing of political rationality or of the degree of support which a proposal engenders takes place at a locus of decision or political arena. Where this center of activity is located within or among political institutions is related to the kind of access that the activists in an issue have to the governmental machinery. Activists whose basis of support is the locality will focus their energy upon the political institutions where local viewpoints are given particular weight. The arena is also a function of the sort of authority needed to make decisions. If the issue requires the commitment of resources, including more money than local or state governments can comfortably command, national political institutions will have to be invoked in policy making.

Whatever the political arena identified with an issue area, there are important implications for the pattern of politics. The formal and informal rules for decision making in various political institutions operate differentially in distributing influence. The influence of certain interests is favored in some branches while it is minimized in others. Urban interests, for example, have a greater impact in the decisions made by the presidency, as a rule, than in those made by Congress.

On water issues, locally oriented political activists have excellent access at points on all levels of government. State water agencies are focal points in deciding which water projects in the state will be pushed for federal authorization. Because water projects frequently require long-term planning and construction under considerable technical expertise, water agencies within the national administration become active in planning and in negotiating water proposals. As has already been indicated, local pressures find an easy mark in the Army Corps of Engineers and the Bureau of Reclamation. However, because water development projects are expensive and because even if the money is borrowed and will be substantially reimbursed, the borrowing capacity required is very great. In effect, Congress, which retains a hold on the purse strings of the federal treasury, must give its consent. The legislative process does provide points of access for federal and state agencies involved in water and other relevant interests as well. Congress thus provides a fairly complete framework for testing the political rationality of a project.

Moreover, of all the political arenas in national government in which policy is made, the legislature is best adapted to the demands of geographic minorities. Local support can be the basis for securing broad backing more easily in Congress than in any other branch of the national government. The local orientation of members of Congress has already been mentioned. And the method of representation, particularly in the Senate, favors areas concerned with water development. For example, the eight Rocky Mountain states in which many reclamation projects are located have sixteen of the 100 senators while they possess less than 4 percent of the population. In addition, the committee system and the informal rules of specialization and seniority favor the local representative in decision making. It is to be expected, then, that the impact of Congress upon water projects is especially marked.

The work of Congress is parceled out in subject matter packets and given to the various committees of the House and the Senate. On most issues, the real work is done in committee. The Public Works committees and the Interior and Insular Affairs committees have most of the jurisdiction over water matters. The makeup of these committees tends to be biased toward the representatives who will benefit most from involvement in the subjects assigned to these committees. For example, more than one-half of the membership of the House Committee on Interior and Insular Affairs came from the seventeen western states during the period between 1947 and 1968.[12] Committee consent, then, need not come from a cross-section of Congress but only from a collection of representatives who generally share constituency concern with water development.

Specialization is an accepted folkway in both the House and the Senate.[13] Since not all members of Congress can be active on every issue, there is a tendency for each to become an expert in particular areas. Other members accept the recommendations of these specialists in policy areas where the specialists are reputed to have expertise. Locally oriented congressional activists on water issues presume the specialists should make the decisions on their side when they have regularly invested time and energy on water matters.

In Congress, localities with senior representatives can have influence in policy out of all proportion to their population. The members who are returned time after time eventually become the committee chairs and the committee leaders. Committee chairs have impressive powers. They are in an excellent position to further constituency interests. Ranking majority and minority members have lesser but still considerable power to act for their constituencies.

Consent-Building Relations

In our constitutional political system, for a proposal to become policy it must be legitimated through the formal action of the political institutions which have authority to make decisions. Such action involves establishing relations among the people and groups with power in these political institutions in such a way as to create consent. These relations vary according to the locus of decision and the formal and informal rules for decision making in the institutions at the locus. For example, consent may be created in the administration by a directive from the chief executive where he has clear authority and influence to act. The relationship here is one of command. Of course, in many circumstances and on many issues, the president lacks such authority and influence, and consent-building relations are then matters of bargaining and persuasion.[14] When the locus of decision is Congress and congressional committees, majority coalitions built up by bargaining relations are required for consent.

The sort of consent-building relations on specific issues also depends on the nature of the issue and actors involved. For instance, where the issue is one in which many persons and groups from a wide range of interests feel a stake, then the consent-building relations will be cooperation on the basis of mutual interests in large coalitions. In such cases, the policy-making process pits giant armies against each other in a struggle for the majority.

The central imperative which structures the relations among actors in water policy is that local support for a project must somehow be projected into national consent. Activists must relate to one another and to others who have influence in the congressional arena in such a way as to broaden their basis of support. Such relations are affected by the fact that advocates of projects in different localities have little perception of shared interest except the common ambition for authorization of various projects. Representatives of areas without the prospect of projects have no immediate incentive to join coalitions backing water development.

The basis of the combinations built to achieve consent for water development is mutual noninterference. This is pork barrel in the purest sense, for a pork barrel is a container of unrelated items. This is not a coalition forged on the basis of shared interest but rather a combination in which members have little in common.[15] Mutual accommodation is one aspect of noninterference and, where it aids in consent building, project proposals which have no connection other than offering local backing are strung together for mutual support. Another aspect of noninterference is the absence of any sort of ends-means analysis. The inclusion of a particular project in a package depends upon its effect on the balance of support and opposition to the package, not upon the relationship of the project to any aims or goals established for water development in general or for the particular collection of projects.

In a pattern of consent building through noninterference, the drive for authorization of a project must come from the locality and from local activists. Commitment and unity within the locality is practically a prerequisite for broadening support. A united stand by the congressional delegation from the state in which a project is located is usually also a necessity. Representatives from both parties and from all factions in a state ordinarily respond to the imperatives of the political process by joining forces.

Local support, even when it is united and even when localities combine behind a package of projects, is not sufficient to create congressional majorities without the consent of representatives from areas without a stake. Relations of noninterference must extend beyond the locally based activists. Such an extension is promoted by the congressional folkways of courtesy, reciprocity, and bargaining. According to the informal rules, representatives and senators are not supposed to obstruct each other, especially when they have little at stake. Caring for future influence implies avoiding making unnecessary enemies. In fact, courtesy dictates that members of Congress help each other when they can. Members are expected by colleagues to be reasonable and willing to bargain.[16] These folkways are especially operative where issues do not divide legislators along party lines.

Locally based activists employ a number of majority-building arguments to acquire the consent of persons and groups with little at stake. Support is justified by magnifying the need and benefits of water projects. It is claimed that projects will foster all sorts of goals, grandiose or particular, even if these goals may be contradictory. Accomplishments of projects are predicted to be water supply for industrial and residential use, flood control, recreation, pollution abatement, fish and wildlife enhancement, and power generation, among other things. Economic and social advantage is promised to all sorts of groups, even if their interests conflict. Reclamationists, recreationists, businessmen and developers, builders, power users, urban and rural water consumers, and Indians and other minority groups may all be appealed to.

Crisis in terms of water scarcity or floods is exploited to create consent.[17] Backers of projects claim that an emergency situation exists. Projects are said to be essential to economic survival. Without water development, the rhetoric goes, the land will return to desert or wash away, as the case may be. At the very least, it is asserted that continued economic growth of a locality hinges upon the particular development being pushed.

In an effort to broaden support, expert testimony from economists, geologists, hydrologists, et al., is collected and cited as firm technical justification for projects. Projects are made to pass experts' tests even if there is little agreement among experts on the soundness of these tests. Whatever its limitations as a scientific test, benefit/cost analysis can be manipulated with a flexibility very useful in building support. Two projects may be joined so that both qualify when one, standing alone, could not. Costs and benefits may be juggled, or the categories may be so extended that almost any project qualifies.[18] As Herbert Marshall puts it, "One of the principal uses of benefit-cost analysis is to clothe politically desirable projects in the fig leaf of economic respectability." [19] Given the leeway which the tool affords activists, it is no wonder that even though the limitations of the test are acknowledged privately, it is faithfully employed and cited.

To facilitate the creation of consent, a project or combination of projects are presented as self-sustaining or money making. Reimbursement has traditionally been a part of reclamation projects. As repayment has for numerous reasons become more and more difficult, the time span in which the government's construction costs must be made up has been continually extended—repayment periods have been lengthened, and development periods have been added on to repayment periods.[20] Increasing amounts of nonreimbursable benefits have also been claimed. The facade of repayment, however, has been maintained. Power generation is often cited as a profit-making feature of projects, although to show a profit, a low government interest rate on power facilities construction funds must often be charged, and a high price for power sales must be anticipated.

Conflict must be avoided or contained if relations of mutual noninterference are to be the basis of building support. A number of tools are employed in water politics to prevent clashes and confrontations. Routinization of the authorization process renders somewhat automatic decisions on which projects to accept and which to act on first. Reclamation projects, for example, are routed through a series of hurdles which must be successfully negotiated before Congress authorizes them. A reconnaissance study establishes the probable feasibility of the project before Congress authorizes a full-scale feasibility study. Once a project is studied and found feasible by the Bureau of Reclamation, it ordinarily must be recommended by the Office of Management and Budget. All these requirements establish a kind of pipeline of projects coming up to Congress in a fashion and order which avoids conflict. Reaching the end of the series of hurdles is also a test of the strength of local backing since real drive is required to move a project along.

At various junctures along the pipeline, projects are required to meet certain technical tests of engineering and economics in order to move forward. The usefulness of one of these tests, benefit/cost analysis, to support building has already been alluded to. It can also be employed to avoid conflict. The technique provides routine criteria for turning down projects, often using public interest explanations with localities.[21] Projects which do manage to come before Congress are bolstered with technical justifications that discourage opposition.

Conflict is coped with at successive area levels as a project moves toward authorization. Local unity is projected into agreements among localities within a portion of a basin, and this, in turn, becomes basinwide, eventually evolving into regional consent. Differences are settled at the level closest to the locality rather than widening the conflict. A primary value among actors expressing area interests is to avoid stalemate which blocks the process of building positive national response to water projects.[22]

Conflict is avoided in Congress by not bringing up broad questions of priorities and ultimate goals. These questions are likely to be divisive and conflict generating. Questions of whether a basin should be developed and for what purposes are avoided in favor of such details as number of projects, sizes, and amounts to be spent. Conflicts that do develop between localities over which localities are to develop what water in what order are dealt with by adding projects and benefits.

Where efforts must be made to contain a high degree of controversy, packages of projects can become very large. Projects are strung together one after another as long as each helps to gain support and overcome opposition. The test applied to each project added is whether it supplies more than it detracts from the support essential to the whole package.

When the source of conflict is not locally based activists who can be handled by the distribution of a project or by a benefit which does not threaten any important source of support, then it must be isolated and excluded from the policy-making process if consent is to be achieved. It has already been indicated that the pattern of initiation and formulation of water development proposals is not receptive to activists whose perceptions are oriented more broadly than the locality and whose aims are not focused on construction of specific projects. Involvement, if it occurs, is a negative reaction triggered by perception of the costs which will be inflicted by the projects proposed. If locally based activists cannot offset this cost, they claim it is unreal or irrelevant.

Conservationist and preservationist challenges to water development projects are often the sort which cannot be met by the add-on process through which locally based conflict is usually handled. Therefore, attempts are made to exclude their interests. Conservation-motivated conflict is labeled as alien interference with local prerogative to put its own water to use. Since conservation organizations often have a national rather than a local basis and organization, they are said to be out of touch with the locality and unable to judge benefits and costs. Claims are made that conservationists lack the knowledge and expertise necessary to judge projects that are bolstered by economic and other justifications. The authorization process is pictured as a technical matter which should not be swayed by the emotional viewpoints of conservationists. Finally, the informal norms of Congress are invoked on the side of local activists, and conservationists are accused of being intransigent and unwilling to bargain. Since they are impossible to accommodate, it is justifiable to exclude their interests.

The Policy

The content of policy is directly related to the process from which it evolves. Who is helped and who is hurt by an allocation of values reflects the perceptions and power resources of the various activists engaged in policy making. The sort of water policy which evolves from the pattern of politics described above is consistent with the pattern. Water policy is plural and responsive to a wide range of local demands. It has many internal contradictions and inconsistencies. It is not reflective of any values about water development other than growth and population expansion. Rather, goals are adjusted according to various specific projects which are included in policy. This kind of policy reinforces the local view of water. It is a bundle of benefits distributed to the localities which have demanded their turn at water development and their fair share of water.

4

The Colorado River Basin Act:
A Water Development Spectacular

Introduction

New Mexico was a minor actor cast in a sideshow of a much larger production in terms of the content of the Colorado River Basin Act and the
political activity involved in its authorization. In a variety of forms, the bill
was scrutinized by Congress for over five years. During that period, some
major portions of the proposal were deleted, and other parts were tacked
on. Complex negotiations preceded each stage of the evolution of the bill.
Some bargains struck were subsequently altered or abandoned and replaced by new agreements. The claims made by New Mexico were ultimately only a few among a large number that had to be dealt with in the
course of achieving congressional approval.

During the lengthy struggle to pass the bill, all seven of the Colorado
River basin states asserted their individual prerogatives. Intense geopolitical
conflicts arose implicating, beyond the demands of individual states, whole
regions of the West. And in addition, the bill became a subject of nationwide attack by conservation groups. Their vigorous campaign generated
literally thousands of letters a week to members of Congress, the president, and the Interior Department during the height of the controversy.

In its final form, the $1.3 billion bill authorized the most expensive rec-
lamation package ever to be approved by Congress in a single stroke. The
core item in the bill, the Central Arizona Project, carried what was then
the record-breaking price tag of $779 million. Water was to be taken from
Lake Havasu, just above Parker Dam, lifted about 900 feet, and transported
via the Granite Reef aqueduct to a reservoir twenty miles from Phoenix.
A series of reservoirs and dams were to conduct water from that point
southwest to the Tucson area. In terms of the degree of controversy, the
ambition of some of the projects within it, and its size, the Colorado River
Basin Act was a spectacular piece of water development legislation.

The Source of Initiative

Arizona was the moving force behind the Colorado River Basin Act.

President Johnson signing the Colorado River Basin Project Act, September 30, 1968. *Visible left to right:* "Bizz" Johnson, Don Clausen, H. Allen Smith, George Murphy, John Rhodes, Carl Hayden, Stewart Udall, Sam Steiger, Lady Bird Johnson, John Saylor, Lyndon B. Johnson, Paul Fannin, Clinton P. Anderson, Thomas Kuchel, Tom Foley, "Mo" Udall, and Ray Elson.

Photo from Special Collections, University of Arizona Library.

Congressman Morris K. Udall, Democrat from Arizona and one of the key congressional activists, observed that the bill was an intensely Arizonan issue. The bill did not have the same sort of emotional impact anywhere else in the basin. Other states had reasons to lend support, but only Arizona had the really compelling determination to achieve authorization.[1]

Arizona's clear and long-standing commitment to federal construction of the CAP initiated the action for a basin bill. Her firm and repeated demand for the project forced other interests to assess their stake in new water development on the Colorado River. A Central Arizona Project bill had first been introduced by Arizona's Senator Ernest W. McFarland in 1947. The CAP had passed the Senate but not the House in both 1950 and 1951. The possibility that Arizona might take substantial amounts of water out of the mainstream of the Colorado had aroused the fears of California about the available quantity to be left downstream. Disagreements between Arizona and California as to the share of water each state was allotted under the Colorado River Basin Compact of 1922 and other laws of the river had resulted in the suspension of congressional action after 1951, and a twelve-year lawsuit in which more testimony was taken than in any previous case ever to come before the Supreme Court. Between 1960 and 1963, anticipation of a Supreme Court decision favorable to Arizona and the renewal of efforts for the CAP had prompted entrepreneurship of representatives of the states in the basin and the Department of the Interior to formulate a plan acceptable to the entire basin.[2]

The energy which had sustained and would continue to sustain the bill in the face of postponement and defeat was also focused in Arizona. Arizonans took up leadership roles in shepherding a basin bill through the congressional maze each session during which the legislation was at issue. They frequently inaugurated bargains and compromises in search of increased support. According to Congressman Udall, the basic strategy of Arizonans was to exploit the self-interest of others with influence in the legislative process by linking in one way or another their plans and desires to the success of the CAP.[3]

The strength and perseverance of Arizona's drive resulted, at least in part, from the unity which existed within the state as to the desirability of the project. In both the major newspapers of Tucson and Phoenix, the Central Arizona Project was a prominent feature of news analyses, editorial pages, and letters to the editor from 1965 until the project was authorized in 1968. Substantially all the coverage was in favor of the project.[4] Whatever doubts were expressed by Arizonans about the need for or the justification of the project were met with stiff rebukes. The *Arizona Review,* published by the University of Arizona, printed an article by two agricultural economists, Robert Young and William Martin, in early 1967, in which they asserted that Arizona had enough groundwater to last 170 years and that redistribution of water from agriculture to municipal and industrial uses was preferable to the CAP. The *Arizona Daily Star* in Tucson, in several editorials, accused the economists of advocating water cannibalism in suggesting reallocation and chided that "the best bet for Tucson and the state is a new source of water, and a great deal less noise."[5] In spite of the atmosphere of fervor within the state, a few groups from Arizona, mostly conservation oriented, testified before congressional committees against portions of the Colorado River bill. Congressman Udall voiced the predominant sentiment in Arizona when he retorted, "I think you people have done our state a disservice."[6] To erase any impression that all Arizona conservation groups objected to the bill, Congressman Udall inserted into the 1965 record the endorsement of the Arizona Conservation Council composed of fifteen organizations.[7]

Arizona officialdom stood together in support of the CAP. The Arizona congressional delegation worked together on the bill, and the three House members, representing both political parties, frequently issued joint press releases. Congressman Udall stated that on this issue he could call on the expertise in Arizona from every agency and group on any level.[8] Both Democratic and Republican governors endorsed the bill. Early in 1966, a task force of Arizonans gathered in Washington to lend advice and support to the efforts of the congressional delegation. The delegates were members and staff of the Arizona Interstate Stream Commission, Arizona Public Service, the Salt River Project, and the Central Arizona Project Association. This group labored continuously until authorization was achieved in 1968.

The extent of Arizona's effort was commensurate with the perceptions within the state of the benefits to be gained from the CAP. This was based partly on the felt need for additional water in some parts of the state. In large part, however, the belief in the CAP was emotional and symbolic.

Without doubt, underground aquifers supplying 80 percent of the water in Arizona were being mined. As the water table declined, the pumping costs to Arizona farmers rose steeply. Some farmers no longer found their crops economically viable. Arizona agriculturists wanted a source of cheaper water. Municipalities recurrently experienced concerns about sufficient supplies to satisfy future growth. Consequently, city governments looked with great favor on the CAP as a source of new water. The Central Arizona Project Association, formed in 1946, represented the interests who believed they would profit directly from the project. Irrigation district, industrial, professional, agricultural, financial, and business interests all contributed to some extent to the expressed intention of obtaining water for Arizona's agricultural economy.[9]

Beyond specific demands, the CAP was an affirmation of the boom which Arizona had been experiencing, particularly since World War II. Optimism within the state about its future came to hinge upon approval of the project. Residents believed the state would come to a standstill or retrogress unless the project were built. Expressing this conviction, Senator Fannin, Republican of Arizona, said on the day of the CAP's passage, "It remains now for the words on paper to be translated into tangible projects giving water and life to Arizona."[10]

Outside any concern with concrete benefits, the achievement of the Central Arizona Project appeared to Arizonans to be their just due. The historical role of Arizona in development of the Colorado River had been neither successful nor satisfying, and Arizonans retained a sense of deprivation and bitterness. Mesmerized by Fred Colter's great dreams of diverting very large amounts of Colorado River water to a great agricultural empire in Arizona, the state had failed to ratify the Colorado River Basin Compact of 1922 that divided water between the upper and lower basins at Lees Ferry in northern Arizona. From then on, the state had fiercely fought the ongoing water development in California which, she envisioned, was pirating her water. Arizona had unsuccessfully petitioned the Supreme Court three times to halt California projects and grant Arizona a more favorable division of water than under the compact.

At last, in 1944, the state made an about face, ratified the compact, and contracted with the secretary of the interior for Arizona's entitlement to 2.8 million acre-feet under the compact. At the same time, the state contracted with the Bureau of Reclamation for an investigation of the uses of Colorado River water. The bureau's ultimate report had provided the outlines of the CAP put before Congress in 1948. At this point, California had disputed Arizona's entitlement, and the famous long lawsuit mentioned heretofore, *Arizona v. California,* ensued. In 1964, the Supreme Court decision gave Arizona a legal right to put to use her 2.8 million acre-feet. However, this paper decree still had to be translated into congressional approval of the CAP.

Looking toward the congressional support necessary for Arizona's project, representatives of the state donned the role of friends of river basin development. Arizonans aided the big upper basin package of projects, the Colorado River Basin Storage Project Act in 1956. The state's spokesmen regularly lent backing to individual state proposals such as the San Juan–Chama project in New Mexico which passed Congress in 1962. In light of the past, Arizonans simply felt they deserved the CAP.

The Core Activists

The whole atmosphere surrounding the CAP proposal in Arizona created powerful incentives for locally based political actors to push some sort of CAP through Congress. The Arizona Interstate Stream Commission, a state agency created in 1948 to prosecute the state's claims to Colorado River water in Congress and before the courts, helped to create and perpetuate this favorable consensus.[11] And throughout the long struggle, the Arizona congressional delegation remained in close touch with this pressure. Indeed, Senator Carl Hayden, the Democrat who had represented Arizona in Congress since statehood, personally shared many of Arizona's humiliations in water politics and looked on the authorization of the CAP as the capstone of his career. The senator and his politically ambitious administrative assistant, Roy Elson, put such stock in the bill that Hayden used his position as chairman of the Senate Appropriations Committee and cashed in a number of accumulated credits among colleagues to further its passage. Congressman John Rhodes, Republican from the Phoenix area, committed huge chunks of time and large portions of the influence he possessed as ranking Republican of the House Appropriations Subcommittee on Public Works to push the bill along. He and Congressman Morris Udall, the latter's constituency including Tucson, maintained a close association throughout the battle. In spite of his reputation for charm and talent, Udall kept his position on the not very prestigious House Interior Committee, presumably to better serve Arizona's water interests. Very frequently in the course of the bill's consideration, Udall

47

fashioned the agreements and compromises that added bulk and potential support to the bill. Other members of the Arizona congressional delegation during this period had less influence and contributed less but were no less vocally committed to the CAP.

The fact that Secretary of the Interior Stewart Udall was an Arizonan affected his perceptions of stakes in the Colorado River Basin Act. He shared Arizonans' enthusiasm for the project, and during his earlier stint in Congress, he had supported basin water development in expectation of backing for the CAP in return. As secretary, Udall continued to do what he could to smooth the way for authorization. In 1962 Secretary Udall informally encouraged Congressman Wayne Aspinall, Democrat of Colorado and chairman of the House Interior and Insular Affairs Committee, to request the department to conduct a comprehensive study of water development on the Colorado River in preparation for the expected pressure for authorization of individual state projects as soon as the decision in *Arizona v. California* was handed down.[12] This gave legislative clearance to department studies already under way. Through the plan, the secretary tried to harmonize divergent interests behind a combination of projects.

In August 1963, the Pacific Southwest Water Plan (PSWWP) was sent to the seven basin states and to five federal departments for review. The overall design attempted to provide supplementary water for multiple use in the whole area of the lower Colorado River basin. No state with entitlements to water below Lees Ferry was neglected, and seven of the seventeen projects proposed specifically benefited Arizona, Nevada, California, New Mexico, and Utah. Particular attention was given in the plan to unifying the interests of Arizona and southern California. A water transfer program was designed to bring water from northern to southern California, and water salvage and reclamation programs were intended to ease some of California's concern for augmenting water supplies to offset withdrawals by the CAP. Common interests were exploited in the PSWWP proposal of two huge hydroelectric dams, Bridge and Marble, to be located in the Grand Canyon. Power revenue was to underwrite the cost of the whole plan and of the future development necessary to guarantee the continued growth of the Southwest.

Secretary Udall lost some of the initiative in the building of a package which would generate broad support when the focus of activity on the bill transferred to Congress. However, throughout the long congressional consideration, Udall acted as a broker among competing interests when the opportunity presented itself. For instance, the secretary acted as a mediator between Arizona and California in negotiations to work out some sort of guarantee to California of 4.4 million acre-feet of water annually—from the Colorado.[13]

The secretary continually exerted pressure for a bill with the CAP. When the 1966 version of the bill failed to get through Congress, the secretary initiated a restudy of the contents of the bill and placed his influence behind a package streamlined to avoid controversy.

In supporting the passage of the basin bill, the secretary was in tune with the interests of the largest unit within his department, the Bureau of Reclamation. The bureau had a tremendous stake in the authorization of the bill. It had participated in the planning of most of the projects proposed in the bill, and its role in putting together the PSWWP had been a central one. The bureau was to be assigned the task of construction and operation of projects. Consequently, the bill represented for the bureau an ongoing mission with funds and personnel.

The bureau's hopes for a bright future for itself were particularly pinned to the Bridge and Marble Canyon dams. These two great structures were to be built on the two remaining best dam sites on the Colorado River. For some time, the bureau had been experiencing difficulty in finding good projects which met economic feasibility criteria.[14] These two projects were moneymakers on paper, and they held particular glamour for the dam-building engineers in the bureau.

Associated with the bureau's concern for the well-being of the agency was its sensitivity to local interests and pressures. The regional office of the bureau was located in Phoenix, and many bureau officials were Arizonans in the sense that they shared the spirit for the CAP. The construction of the Central Arizona Project was an essential part of the relationship which locally based bureau officials had worked out with water agencies in Arizona. In consequence of these and other interests, the bureau actively worked for the Colorado River Basin Act in the administration, in Congress, and in other public forums. Experts within the bureau regularly loaned their talents to the Arizona congressional delegation and other influential people.

Building Support

Achieving congressional approval of the Colorado River Basin Act required the creation of a majority at a number of stages in the legislative process: House and Senate subcommittees with jurisdiction over reclamation projects, the full House and Senate committees on Interior and Insular Affairs, the House Rules Committee, the floor of the House and the Senate, and the conference committee. A variety of activists inside and outside the basin perceived a stake in the bill and possessed resources in one or more of these settings. These concerns had to be accommodated or overcome if all the hurdles in the congressional process were to be successfully negotiated.

Looking at the legislative situation in September of 1966, Morris Udall saw a number of power centers to be attended to, some necessary and others not indispensable sources of support. Among the absolutely necessary supporters of the bill, Udall counted Congressman Aspinall,

Senator Henry Jackson, Democrat from Washington, and Senator Clinton P. Anderson, Democrat from New Mexico, along with Senator Hayden and the administration.[15]

Crucial Supporters

Congressman Aspinall was placed in the category of vital support because of his position as chairman of the substantive committee with jurisdiction over the Colorado River basin bill. His power resources as chairman and his habit of putting them to use made him a force with which to contend. As chairman he exercised firm control over the agenda of the committee. Bills were considered when Chairman Aspinall decided they should be considered. As chairman he wielded yet another tool, that of timing. He decided when the committee would convene outside the usual Wednesday meetings. He determined when the committee would adjourn for the session. As chairman, Aspinall appointed the members of subcommittees and subcommittee chairmen, and exercised additional powers including control over staff appointments and considerable authority over the uses to which staff time would be put. As chairman, he might structure hearings and schedule the witnesses.

The interests which motivated Congressman Aspinall in the use he made of his power on the Colorado River basin bill were mixed and complex. He was the champion of the state of Colorado and the particular spokesman of the western slope in water matters. His role also included a more general paternity of the whole Colorado River basin and a felt responsibility for peaceful and harmonious development of water resources. As a committee chairman, he was necessarily attentive to the degree of unity his committee could muster, its ability to make decisions and exert influence, and the reputation of his committee in Congress as a whole.

The role of Chairman Aspinall vis-à-vis Colorado and the western slope was to assert and protect water claims. The hard fact was that the water supply in the river, although uncertain, was definitely not sufficient to satisfy every state's entitlement on paper. On the assumption that the river contained at least 15 million acre-feet per year, the Colorado River Compact had determined that the upper basin must deliver to Lees Ferry an average of 7.5 million acre-feet of water annually over a ten-year period. By statute and judgment of the Supreme Court, California was entitled to 4.4 million acre-feet. California, in fact, has used far more than this. The Mexican water treaty assuring 1.5 million acre-feet to our neighbor to the south also had to be satisfied. Although entitled to 2.8 million acre-feet of water, Arizona's use of this amount through the CAP could not be accomplished without cutting sharply into water supplies legally earmarked for the upper basin but not yet developed.

Once upper basin water, of which Colorado has had the largest share, was put to use in the lower basin, Congressman Aspinall and other upper basin representatives had reason to fear it would never be retrieved. Development would require federal financing. Once California and Arizona were using upper basin water, they were likely to be loath to cut back. The support of these states for upper basin projects in the future was far from certain. To protect Colorado's water, Congressman Aspinall needed to ensure authorization of projects putting Colorado's full entitlement to use. Augmentation of the river would also ensure upper basin water claims.

During his lengthy tenure in Congress going back to 1948, Congressman Aspinall had presided over the passage of a great deal of reclamation legislation and the authorization of a number of projects in the Colorado River basin. He had accumulated a stake over the years in seeing development of the basin move forward. Prospects for the future, at this point in time, had become associated with satisfactorily dealing with Arizona's demand for the CAP. Congressman Aspinall had an interest in handling the controversy in such a way that the whole basin could continue to exploit the river with federal help.

Congressional committees have always varied tremendously in the respect and influence they command on Capitol Hill, and committee chairs have had an obvious interest in a high rating. A number of factors have made for a good reputation for a congressional committee, including the quality of its members and the importance of its jurisdiction. Committees which treat their subject matter with expertise and display a high degree of cohesion have tended to be more prestigious and more successful in getting committee bills through the floor. Congressman Aspinall had an interest in avoiding committee conflict on the Colorado River Basin Act. He expressed his viewpoint in advice given to Arizona leaders in September of 1964:

> Finally, I cannot emphasize enough the importance of unity within Arizona and agreement among the five states, and especially Arizona and California. My committee and the Congress have been following a policy of not deciding differences within a state and hesitate to consider a basin water development program when there is a serious controversy between or among the states involved. The problems of successfully moving a large reclamation program through the House of Representatives are so great under the best of conditions that the addition of a serious intrabasin controversy would present a very difficult task.[16]

The chairman's stake in his committee's reputation committed him to turning out a competent piece of legislation in terms of economics and engineering which would do credit to the committee on the floor. He insisted that plans conform to established committee policies and criteria and be authorized through regular procedure. For example, in projects proposed he was determined to meet the basic professional requirement that there be a sure source of water.

Senator Henry Jackson was Aspinall's counterpart in the Senate, and his command as committee chairman made him a figure the Arizona activists on the Colorado River Basin Act had to satisfy. Like Aspinall, Jackson was concerned with the interest of his area. In addition, he was more broadly attentive to the progress and direction of natural resource development. He was as concerned as the House chairman with relationships on the Senate Committee on Interior and Insular Affairs and its stature on the floor.

The interests of Washington and the rest of the Northwest became implicated in the Colorado River Basin Act as a package of proposals took form which combined the interests of the seven basin states but presented certain threats. Augmentation of the Colorado River promised relief from pressure and conflicts among the basin states. Both the upper basin representatives and Californians came to pin their hopes for relief from shortages made worse by the CAP upon importation from the Columbia River. At one point, interbasin transfer of eight million acre-feet or more was contemplated. Many of the states in the Northwest were engaged in studying their water resources, but were not to the point of admitting to any kind of water surplus available for transfer to the Southwest. Senator Jackson became acutely aware of a stake in the Columbia, whole and undiminished.

The concern for possible damage to the Northwest arising from the Colorado River Basin Act awakened Senator Jackson to the whole issue of reclamation and water development. He became convinced that a number of choices important to the nation were being made in terms of allocation of water resources and that these deserved a national focus and national study.[17]

Senator Jackson's committee had a reputation for harmony and expert craftsmanship in legislation.[18] The senator had a stake in protecting this in regard to the Colorado River Basin Act. The CAP and associated projects had to be handled in a way that would unite as many as possible in the committee without raising a ruckus on the floor. One of the important considerations here was Senator Hayden and the enormous bank of goodwill he had accumulated over his half-century in Congress. The strictures of the inner club of the Senate strongly pressured Jackson, and his committee had to give Hayden the CAP, a project Hayden regarded as his final contribution to Arizona.

Senator Clinton Anderson provided an additional power point in the Senate for the Arizona activists to contend with. The senator held certain authority as chairman of the Power and Reclamation Subcommittee. More important, however, was the stature of the man himself. His immense reputation in Congress, the administration, and among groups concerned with water development, magnified his influence far beyond the subcommittee. Further, his particularly close relationship to Senator Jackson made accommodation with Senator Anderson a requisite to a meeting of minds with the full committee chairman.[19]

Senator Anderson's particular stake in the Colorado River Basin Act will be thoroughly explored in chapters 5 and 6, dealing with Hooker Dam. It is sufficient in this context to note that the senator from New Mexico was anxious to protect and even extend the entitlement of his state to basin water.

Senator Hayden and the administration could be counted as activists for Arizona. Perceptions of stakes diverged sufficiently from the House activists, however, that they were mentioned by Congressman Udall as power centers who had to be satisfied for Arizona to get a bill. Senator Hayden and some members of his staff took a strict line in regard to California. It was felt that Arizona had won a great victory in *Arizona v. California*. Any sort of guarantee in the legislation which would provide that California need not share the burden of shortages below her basic entitlement of 4.4 million acre-feet was, in the view of people in Hayden's office, giving away the Supreme Court winnings.

Secretary Udall faced within the administration certain pressures which distinguished him as an activist from his brother and his brother's colleagues in the House. Within his department was the Park Service and the Bureau of Outdoor Recreation and other organizations which saw dams, especially near or within national parks, as a threat. Even when these units could be quieted, the constituencies they represented could have an impact elsewhere in the administration.

The Bureau of the Budget, later to be expanded and renamed the Office of Management and Budget, was sensitive for the president to controversies which could arouse a wide public concern, such as the Grand Canyon dams. Budget, pressed with the problem of national budget priorities, took a harsh view of project feasibility. Indeed, outside the Bureau of Reclamation and the secretary, there was little positive commitment to the CAP within the administration. The upshot was that the secretary had to back versions of the CAP which did not arouse general controversy if he were to bring the administration with him.

Other Power Centers

From the vantage point of Congressman Udall, committed to pushing some sort of CAP bill through the legislative gauntlet, there were a number of power centers to attend to which he viewed as important, but depending upon the way various supporters combined behind the bill, not really crucial.

The potential influence and considerable interest which California had in the bill made it worthy of attention from the Arizona-based activists. California commanded impressive power within the structure of Congress. California claimed five members of the House Interior and Insular Affairs

Committee, all of whom were members of the Subcommittee on Irrigation and Reclamation, and during part of the House's consideration of the basin bill, Harold T. (Bizz) Johnson, Democrat of California, was chairman of the subcommittee. California had two votes on the House Rules Committee and held thirty-eight votes on the House floor.

Senator Kuchel, Republican of California, was ranking minority member of the Senate Committee on Interior and Insular Affairs and shared some of Chairman Jackson's prerogatives. In addition, he had some influence in the Senate as a whole, as indicated by his position as whip for the Republican party in the Senate.

The central concern of California about the Colorado River Basin Act was water supply to serve its burgeoning population and the elaborate waterworks already constructed in the southern part of the state. The 1967 use by California of Colorado River water was well over 5 million acrefeet, while the Supreme Court's interpretation of the law allotted it only 4.4 million acre-feet. The construction of the CAP implied a cutback in California uses. Her representatives wanted assurances that at least the 4.4 million would be guaranteed for California. If shortages arose so that the full 7.5 million acre-feet allotted to Arizona, Nevada, and California were not available, then California did not want to share in the shortage. In addition, California hoped that the aqueduct size of the CAP would be small enough to minimize its drafts from the river.

Since matters of water rights made shortages fall first upon the Los Angeles–San Diego megalopolis, California was desperately in search of new water. Northern California promised one source and transfers were contemplated in the Pacific Southwest Water Plan, but the supply was not large enough. The Columbia River came to be the focus of California's hopes, and she was anxious to get on with a study demonstrating the feasibility of such interbasin transfers. The project foretokened huge expense. Californians looked toward the large hydroelectric dams, Bridge (renamed Hualapai) and Marble, to help supply revenues to a fund large enough for such an undertaking.

Utah and Wyoming, the upper basin states not already dealt with here, were also sources of minor concern for the Arizona activists. These two states shared many of Colorado's misgivings about the CAP. They worried for fear their water could not be retrieved from the lower basin when they were ready to put it to use. Importation, for these two upper basin states, appeared the only sure way to protect their entitlement.

Although their concern was intense, Utah and Wyoming lacked the power to express it effectively. Their representation in Congress was small and not placed in important positions such as committee chairs. They exercised some influence through the Upper Colorado River Basin Commission which represented the four upper basin states and recommended legislation. However, Colorado and New Mexico, although members of the commission, felt free to take independent positions, thus weakening the commission's influence. To be really influential, Utah and Wyoming had to hold some sort of balance of power at a stage in the legislative process.

Another center of power, estimated as dispensable by Congressman Udall and consequently probably underestimated by Arizona activists, was conservation. The conservation movement in the 1960s was a fragmented collection of organizations representing interests as divergent as hunters and defenders of wildlife. They varied in size from several million members to several thousand. Among this collection were a few militant groups who sensed a great deal to lose in the inclusion of hydroelectric dams in the Colorado River Basin Act. The Sierra Club was most prominent of these groups. A California-based organization, the Sierra Club had a nationwide membership of about 40,000 at the time of the Grand Canyon battle. Its talented and controversial executive director, David Brower, the club's Southwest representative, other members of the staff, and the board of directors, committed time, energy, and financial resources to fight dams in the vicinity of the Grand Canyon. The influence of the organization was magnified many times above the size of its membership by the intensity of its feelings, the emotional impact of its message, and its access to the national press.

The conservationist stake in blocking dams in the Grand Canyon was partly love of the place. To many who had been there and to some who had only heard about it or seen the Sierra Club exhibit format book of full-color photographs, *Time and the River Flowing*, the living heart of the Grand Canyon was the free-flowing river. It did not matter that rim tourists would probably not even see a reservoir or dam site. If the river which carved the canyon no longer worked its geological miracle, the whole canyon would be irretrievably damaged.

Beyond the canyon itself, the battle to prevent dams had other symbolic significance. For militant conservation organizations, at risk were the scenic resources of the nation and the national park system. A Sierra Club advertisement in the *New York Times* was headed, "Dinosaur and Big Bend. Glacier and Grand Teton, Kings Canyon, Redwoods, Mammoth, Even Yellowstone and Yosemite. And the Wild Rivers and the Wilderness. How Can You Guarantee These, Mr. Udall, If the Grand Canyon Is Dammed for Profit?"[20] It was believed that if the world-renowned Grand Canyon could not be saved from development, nothing could be. The conservationists were immersed in a desperate battle. David Brower frequently remarked that only 10 percent of the earth was left untrammeled by man. Each encroachment on a previously undeveloped area further reduced the small fraction of the planet in which humans could experience the natural world. A compromise of wilderness was an irretrievable loss.

Part of the emotionalism of the conservationists derived from the conviction that the case for the Grand Canyon dams had been stacked. They felt that a whole establishment based on self-interest, mostly economic, justifying its position by incomplete and shortsighted analysis, and intensely intolerant of opposition opinion, was being pitted against them. They claimed that the Bureau of Reclamation, coveting expensive construction projects, biased their recommendations of feasibility. Divergent voices in the administration were being quashed, and diversity of opinion on the dams within Arizona and other basin states was being treated as unpatriotic.

Conservationists had some power at various stages of the legislative process. Congressman John P. Saylor, Republican from Pennsylvania, was ranking minority member of the Interior and Insular Affairs Committee. He had gained the reputation of conservation leadership during consideration of the wilderness bill in 1964. Chairman Aspinall consulted with him to some extent, and his position afforded him excellent openings to make arguments and offer amendments against the dams. Other legislators reputed to be sensitive to conservation issues were scattered among relevant House and Senate committees.

The influence of militant conservation was most impressive on the floor of the House and Senate. This was due partly to the conservation organizations' nationwide lobbying campaign urging people to write, and partly to the sympathetic audience they received from the editorial staff of such major newspapers as the *New York Times* and the *Washington Post*. Letters against the dams deluged many members of Congress who had little interest in the water problems of the Colorado River basin. Besides the massive mail, a number of congressional members were subjected to appeals from influential constituents who were hard to disregard. More than a few members were approached by a long-time supporter who would "never ask for anything for himself," but wanted the member to "do something for the earth, and future generations which would live on it. Do not dam the Grand Canyon."[21]

While Congressman Udall underestimated conservation as a source of influence, he was more attentive to other power centers. These included such specialized groups as public power, private power, The National Mine Workers Union, and other specific associations which had a fairly narrow interest in particular provisions of the Colorado River Basin Act. These groups had some impact on the voting behavior in Congress. Some states such as Texas and Kansas, which were distant from the basin, saw a possible source of additional water for their area during the time when importation was seriously discussed, and their representatives in Congress became, for a while, potential power centers.[22]

Legislative History

In order to vault all the hurdles of the legislative process, the Arizona activists had to combine the support of the various power centers in such a way as to create a majority for the Colorado River Basin Act at each stage of congressional action: House and Senate committees and subcommittees, the House Rules Committee, and the floor of both bodies. The tangled legislative history of the bill can best be understood as a series of efforts to put together a winning combination.

Background of 1966 Action

Arizona began her efforts to translate the victory she had achieved in the Supreme Court into congressional authorization of the CAP by heeding Congressman Aspinall's counsel that the first step was lower basin unity.[23] In exchange for California's assurance of support for the CAP, Arizona agreed to grant California a limited priority in times of shortage on the river. If in any particular year there were to be insufficient water to provide both a full supply for Arizona's aqueduct and California's 4.4. million acre-feet entitlement, the CAP would bear that shortage.

In accord with California's determination to acquire a dependable long-range supply of water sufficient to meet all of the entitlements and continue to support southern California's rapid growth, it was agreed that the bill should contain authorization of immediate feasibility studies of augmentation of the Colorado by all means including interbasin transfer. To pay for the eventual augmentation program, a basin fund would be created largely from revenues from Marble and Bridge (Hualapai) dams. A real financial boost was given to augmentation by making the expense of obtaining the first 2.5 million acre-feet a year, the amount needed to make the Colorado whole, a national obligation.

Nevada was quite willing to contribute to lower basin unity on the basis of the bargains struck between Arizona and California. Implicit in the bargain was the agreement of the other states to support the Southern Nevada Supply bill through which Nevada could put her Colorado River entitlement to use.

These agreements served only as a preliminary step to further bargaining. Provisions attracting support from the upper basin had to be tacked on. The upper basin and the upper basin's most influential representative, Congressman Aspinall, felt there were insufficient guarantees in the bill of upper basin water development in spite of the augmentation provisions which they also wanted. Senator Anderson saw too little in the bill for New Mexico. After many rounds of conferences, an entire seven-state agreement was pounded out.

The upper basin took the opportunity to settle a sore point with the Bureau of Reclamation concerning the filling of Glen Canyon Dam. At certain times in the past, Lake Powell behind Glen Canyon had been drawn down with consequent loss of power-generating capacity in order to fill demands for water and power at Hoover. A complex but mutually agreeable set of criteria for operating dams was established, and the upper basin fund was to be reimbursed for past power losses.

Further, upper basin states insisted on the authorization of a number of projects in the bill to protect their entitlements and to take advantage of the impetus behind the CAP to push ahead their own development. The Dixie Project in Utah was to be reauthorized and integrated in the upper basin fund. Four projects in Colorado and one in Colorado and New Mexico were injected into the bill. New Mexico was to receive the Gila Dam and 18,000 acre-feet of water under an exchange with the CAP.

These along with scores of minor agreements, such as the one with the Hualapai Indians, renaming Bridge Canyon Dam and reimbursing the tribe for the use of the site, were incorporated in a bill which was reported favorably by the House Interior and Insular Affairs Committee in August of 1966. Success in the House committee came only through the mammoth and patient efforts of Congressmen Udall and Rhodes and the consent of the chairman. In the course of hearings and discussions on the 1966 bill, it became obvious that building majorities in other settings on the bill as written was likely to be even more difficult.

The northwesterners on the Interior and Insular Affairs Committee were adamant in their opposition to any kind of study of interbasin transfers which might have as their source the Columbia or its major tributary, the Snake. The Northwest was particularly opposed to a study by the Bureau of Reclamation. They felt that the bureau was already committed to interbasin transfers rather than to other means of augmentation, and that it would be difficult for the bureau to report unfavorably on such a huge project when it would be the bureau itself which would construct the importation works.[24] Northwesterners felt that the cards were stacked against them in a committee led by basin representatives and in which they had only four votes. In such a setting, they could hope to do no more than delay action and upset negotiations.[25] In the Senate, however, the story was different. Senator Jackson held these same views and could block action on a bill that contained the kind of study provisions in the House document.

Anticipating the eventual accommodations necessary to pass the bill, Chairman Aspinall, along with Congressman Walter Rogers of Texas, subcommittee chairman, made an effort during the committee markup to change the study of transfers to meet the objections of the Pacific Northwest. The effort was thwarted by the Californians in combination with some upper basin representatives and by the Arizonans, the latter evidently determined to hold on to their settlement with California.

By August of 1966, the full conservationist campaign was mobilized, and the public concern it generated was being registered by rank and file congressmen. Throughout the summer, the Arizona congressmen and the task force held steak luncheons to gather congressmen's commitments to support the CAP. Congressman Rhodes used his considerable influence as a member of the Appropriations Committee and as the chairman of the Policy Committee of the Republican party in the House to sway votes. Congressman Udall, too, cashed in on a number of accumulated favors done for colleagues. Morris Udall has always been extremely likeable, and many congressmen in both parties wanted to go along with him simply on the basis of friendship.[26] In spite of the persuasiveness of the Arizona campaign, the conservationists cut deeply into the floor support. In the head count tallies kept by the task force, an increasing number of congressmen were reported as wanting to go along, but feeling unable to because of sentiment in their constituencies against the dams. At the last tally done in the 89th Congress, the Arizonans still believed they could count on 167 sure votes and 74 probable supporters. This seemed to be ample support, but the Californians and others remained uncomfortable.[27]

In the closing weeks of the 89th Congress, efforts to obtain a rule from the Rules Committee so that the Colorado River Basin Act could move on to the House floor were abandoned. Determining the motivation is like discovering who killed Cock Robin. The Arizonans blamed the Californians who held two votes on the Rules Committee and were in a position to block action. In their view, California was simply worried about its 4.4 priority and wanted to prevent any amendments from the floor. The Californians believed that there was a strong possibility that a substitute bill could be introduced by Congressman Saylor which would strike the Grand Canyon dams and perhaps augmentation as well as the 4.4. Since Arizona could not give concrete assurance that they had the votes lined up to prevent this, California believed that sending the bill to the floor was too risky. The impetus for pushing the bill was slowed by the knowledge that the Senate probably would not be able to act in the time remaining in the session. The controversy surrounding the terms of the seven-state agreement was such that a bill could not be simply slipped through the Senate side. The upshot was that the Arizonans were faced with the prospect of again beginning the task of constructing sufficient support to pass the CAP through the various divergent power centers.

In late 1966, the core activists in Arizona had second thoughts about the political feasibility of a really large Colorado River basin bill.[28] The congressional delegation and the task force were bent upon a bare-bones Colorado River basin bill with little besides the CAP. Rather than seeking support, the Arizonans determined to start with the minimum, and "let them come to us for a change."[29] In January of 1966, the Arizona delegation in the House introduced a bill with the CAP, only one dam in the Grand Canyon, a reconnaissance rather than feasibility study of augmentation, no upper basin projects, and no priority for California. To backstop congressional efforts, Arizonans seriously set in motion plans for state financing of the CAP.

The misgivings of the Arizonans were echoed in other basin states. The glue which had held the basin combination together was the hope of new water and the creation of a large development fund to pay for it. Once this became of questionable political feasibility, localities were pitted against one another in competition for supplies in a water-short river. About thirty bills were introduced in the House and five in the Senate at the start of the 90th Congress, indicating the disarray of the basin coalition.

Recognizing that some new combination of interests was necessary if the Colorado River basin bill were ever to reach the president's desk, Secretary Udall led the department into some fundamental rethinking. He established a task force composed of technicians of the Bureau of Reclamation, members of his staff, and invited representatives of the Bureau of the Budget. The task force was directed to explore all the alternative approaches to the construction of the CAP without regard to existing law, policy, and institutional restraints.[30]

The secretary's task force came up with over thirty complete project plans, including a variety of altenatives among which were pumped-storage hydroelectric plants and variations in sizes of the mainstream dams. Through a process which cannot be unraveled even by those intimately involved, the secretary in February 1967 chose a single plan which represented a major change in his position. He eliminated the dams from the administration package and provided that the federal government, in part by prepayment of capital costs, obtain low-cost pumping for the Central Arizona Project from coal-fired, thermal power plants built by a consortium of private and public utilities. He proposed no augmentation studies to be directly connected with the CAP, but rather endorsed the separate authorization of the National Water Commission which, he anticipated, would give general consideration to matters of water supply.

The Senate committee acted first in the 90th Congress, and the kind of proposal made by the administration had a particular appeal in that setting. Senator Jackson, aided by Senator Anderson and Senators Church and Jordan of Idaho, were able to effect a majority commanding agreement with Senator Hayden which overrode the strong objections of Senators Thomas Kuchel of California, Gordon Allott of Colorado, and Clifford Hansen of Wyoming. These three senators reflected an opinion strong in some upper basin states and in California that "the only permanent solution is to augment the river's supply."[31] The bill as reported out tried to mollify basin opposition by providing something for everyone: 4.4 million acre-foot priority to California for twenty-seven years, five projects for Colorado, Dixie Project for Utah, and Hooker Dam and a share of Animas–La Plata for New Mexico. At the same time, it accommodated the conservationists and northwesterners with no dams and no augmentation studies. The overall package had such wide appeal that it handily passed the Senate by a vote of 70 to 12.[32]

Building a majority in the House for this Colorado River basin bill required accommodation of Colorado and California representatives whose position as power centers was much more prominent than in the Senate. Chairman Aspinall indicated that the Senate version "sounded the death knell for the session."[33] The control exercised by committee chairs in the 1960s was far greater than they were to have after reforms in the 1970s. In August, Aspinall announced that his committee would adjourn without action beyond the hearings held early in the year. With the momentum gained by Senate passage, however, Arizonans were determined to push for House action.

Arizona activists in Congress engaged in a variety of tactics to pry the bill loose from the chairman's grip. Congressman Udall began by an appeal to the Coloradan himself, explaining the pressures from home to which the Arizona delegation was being subjected. The chairman responded that he would "understand" if a move was made in the committee to override him but that he was going home to Colorado, saying simply, "You will have a hard time meeting without me."[34]

The power structure in the whole House was the focus of yet another appeal. Congressman Udall directed a letter to Speaker John McCormack in which he recounted the long and tortured history of the CAP and the numerous demands made by California and Colorado. Udall reminded the Speaker, head of the House Democratic party, that both he and Senator Hayden would be up for reelection in 1968 and would profit from a CAP victory. Finally, he requested Speaker McCormack to ask Aspinall about the status of the bill and to mention to the chairman the importance of the bill.[35] This evidently was done. Mr. Aspinall responded with a missive to the Speaker in which he told Colorado's side of the issue and his own view of its legislative history. Time, Aspinall wrote, would be necessary to work out an agreement to protect the upper basin.[36]

Pressure was brought to bear on the chairman from points outside the House. Arizonans generated controversy on the western slope by letters to major newspapers in Aspinall's constituency, pointing out all the locality had to gain from the bill, including five water development projects. Editorials appeared in national newspapers critical of the chairman's adjournment decision. The minority leader, Senator Everett Dirksen, expressed disappointment at the chairman's high-handed actions.

Senator Hayden used his position on the Appropriations Committee to threaten to stall construction funds for the Frying Pan–Arkansas project in Colorado and to hold up funds for other propositions important to the House chairman. Later he pushed through his committee a rider attaching the CAP to an appropriations bill.

The accumulated pressures brought Chairman Aspinall back to Washington from Colorado in early October for a special committee meeting. He announced that the CAP would be a priority item at the opening of the next session. This, he said, had been his intention before all the attempts to move him had been made.[37]

Chapter 4

The other balky power center blocking the progress of the CAP bill, the Californians, was also subjected to persuasion. Morris Udall told California leaders in a speech to them in Los Angeles:

I must tell you bluntly that no bill providing for a so-called Grand Canyon Dam can pass the Congress today. . . . I must also tell you that no bill providing for augmentation of the Colorado River by importing water from the Columbia River system—or even feasibility studies directed at the Columbia—can pass the Congress today. . . . Yet the official position of the California water agencies as I stand here at this moment is that the Central Arizona Project must be opposed vigorously unless these two impossible conditions are included. . . . If this is California's position you are simply out to obstruct any Arizona bill from ever passing. . . . We have been promised that early in 1968 there will be a vote in the House Interior Committee on this legislation. We intend to try to win it—either with your help or over your dead bodies.[38]

California had considerable interest in participating in whatever sort of CAP bill was to pass the House. Her central concern was with the 4.4 priority which she had little hope of achieving without supporting the legislation. Further, future progess in reclamation in every state was dependent on overcoming the bottleneck of the CAP. William Gianelli, California's director of water resources appointed by the new Reagan administration, called for a negotiated settlement with Arizona and said California was willing to go halfway. Failure to reach agreement, he told water users in his state, would leave California's entitlement undefined and a definite threat to southern California's future growth.

With a disposition among major actors more favorable to compromise, a series of complex negotiations between basin representatives was undertaken at the start of the second session of the 90th Congress. Bargaining sessions continued through hearings and markup by the House Interior Committee. One agreement after another was struck as the spring of 1968 wore on. The administration's steam plant concept was accepted and both Grand Canyon dams were dropped. A 4.4 priority for California with minor qualifications was written into the bill. The Mexican water treaty obligation to supply water to Mexico was transferred from the seven basin states to the nation. Two Colorado River basin funds were created, one to pay for the CAP and the other, gleaned mostly from revenues produced in California, set aside for augmentation. Congressman Burton, Republican of Utah, managed to wring from the committee a conditional authorization of the Uintah project in Utah. Yet obstacles remained, for the demands of the northwesterners could not be accommodated in the same way. Importation was still essential to protecting entitlements as California and Colorado viewed matters; so provisions for importation were emphatically included. As a further guarantee of Colorado's full development of its water, the five Colorado projects were to be constructed concurrently with the CAP.

The committee majority behind this package of provisions was projected easily through the Rules Committee and onto the House floor. Repeated attacks on the bill by northwesterners and Congressman Saylor, still opposed to many details in the package, were handily rebuffed. House passage was finally achieved on May 16, 1968.

Majority building in the setting of the conference committee required the settling of a geopolitical conflict, the two sides of which were represented by the respective House and Senate chairmen. Senator Jackson found any reference to an augmentation study completely unacceptable. He preferred that the measure not make the Mexican water treaty a national obligation which would involve the national government intimately in solving the problem of water supply on the Colorado. In this setting, Congressman Aspinall's perspective was that of the Southwest, and his role was to keep all sources of new water for the basin open.

One of the keys to the compromise was the disposition of the National Water Commission. The commission bill, upon which Jackson pinned his hopes for a national approach to water problems rather than the existing regional view which had set sights on importation, had been passed by both houses, but in different versions. Working out differences in the appointment of members, mission, jurisdiction, and operation of the commission had to be accomplished while the basin bill held fire. On July 18, a conference committee agreed to National Water Commission language, clearing the way for the CAP.

After six sessions of the conference, agreement was reached. The settlement between the Northwest and Southwest was the major event. A ten-year moratorium on diversion studies was declared, although studies by the secretary of the interior of the long-range water requirements of the Southwest, along with investigations of other means of augmentation, were to proceed. The other part of the basic geopolitical settlement declared the obligation of the Mexican water treaty to be national. When augmentation of the river was achieved, the cost of replacing Mexican deliveries was to be nonreimbursable.

Once this basic bargain was struck between the Northwest and Southwest, all other issues were swept along to quick disposition: a 4.4 guarantee to California in perpetuity and a CAP aqueduct of the size the Arizonans desired, although the state would be required to pay part of the cost.

The conference committee report was approved readily by both houses, although representatives of some upper basin states remained disgruntled. Wyoming, which had been left out when projects were passed around, was most bitter. Utahans also expressed grave reservations on the issue of water supply. Senator Gordon Allott voiced the continuing fear that without guaranteed augmentation, Colorado might be deprived of water apportioned to her but used by the CAP. The concurrent reconstruction provision in the final bill did little to reassure him. These, however, were minority views in an atmosphere of general accord.

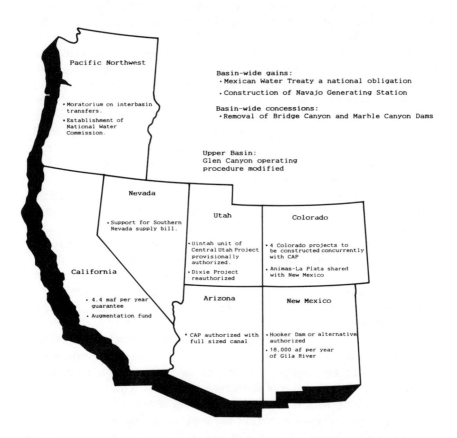

The Geopolitics of the Colorado River Basin Bill: Gains to the States

Overview

To recount the story of the Colorado River Basin Act is like following the construction of a very complex puzzle. The various pieces were different power centers, and the process of putting them together was a matter of delicate negotiation and bargaining. The completed puzzle revealed successful majorities at all stages of the legislative process. Because of the differential influence of various power centers at different stages, a great many pieces had to be attended to. Any center which could block majority building anywhere in the legislative process had somehow to be fitted into the broad agreement. The difficulty of the puzzle was magnified by the fact that only the Arizonans were fundamentally committed to putting the whole thing together. Most other actors were concerned only with the disposition of a few pieces of the puzzle.

The very broad agreement required for successfully ordering all the pieces of the puzzle meant that a number of issues had to be postponed. To settle them would have intensified the job of seeking majorities beyond all possibility of handling. For example, the question of where the water for the CAP was to come from after the year 2020, when all states in the basin will have put their entitlements to work, could not be answered. Some basic matters could not even be considered in this framework. The matter of whether the economic growth of the Southwest should be subsidized by water development built by the nation could not be entertained. To raise such an issue was to threaten the cohesion which made negotiation among different power centers possible at all. Likewise priorities in the use of water and among different projects could not be set. Attempting this would have been to heighten the competition already existing to some extent because of the shortage in the basin. Containing this degree of conflict took mammoth efforts as it was, especially after the relief of diversion did not materialize.

The face of the puzzle as finally completed is a jumbled picture. The Colorado River Basin Act is not a very logical or consistent piece of legislation. It does not establish any overall plan of development; different projects and provisions are not complementary, and some of the bargains arrived at, such as the Mexican Water Treaty burden, appear as rather fantastic dodges from confronting basic problems of supply. The bill can be said to be a spectacular piece of legislation but not because it accomplished any basic innovations in the direction of water development. The really spectacular aspect must be seen as the political accomplishment of fitting together so many divergent interests.

5

The Animas–La Plata:
Reclamation Politics as Usual

Introduction

The Animas–La Plata Project had an excellent chance of eventual authorization even without any sort of association with the Central Arizona Project. The project was advancing along the usual route reclamation projects travel in obtaining congressional approval. Had the issue of a Colorado River basin bill never come up and had the ongoing process of gaining consent at various levels and branches of government been allowed to run its course, the Animas–La Plata Project might well have provided a typical example of the policy-making process in reclamation. Of course, in such event the low visibility of the issue and the lack of real conflict involved would probably have discouraged anyone from writing a case history.

Only to a point, however, was Animas–La Plata a routine authorization. The advent of a Colorado River basin bill and its association with the Animas–La Plata Project had the effect of wrenching the timing of the policy-making process. Since time can often be a political resource, the change in the schedule somewhat distorted the distribution of power from what it ordinarily would have been. This, in turn, was reflected in the content of the project finally approved by Congress along with the CAP.

As the subsequent history of Animas–La Plata outlined in chapter 9 shows, the status of a low-visibility, routine reclamation project was never to be recaptured. Association with the Colorado River Basin Act probably worked to delay rather than hasten construction, and with each passing year came more impediments and doubts. There was not even a shadow of the misgivings that were later to be expressed by some locals when the project was initiated.

Initiatives on the Project

The genesis of the Animas–La Plata Project can be traced back at least to 1938, although as long as farming has been an occupation in the La Plata basin, a dependable supply of water has been ardently desired. In that year, the Bureau of Reclamation formulated a plan to transfer water from the Animas River to the La Plata River in the San Juan basin of Colorado.[1] Some revisions were made to this basic proposal in 1966, but the 1938 plan had remained substantially unaltered.

The initiative for the project derived from local water users in the La Plata areas of Colorado and New Mexico, but especially in Colorado. The La Plata Water Conservancy District had been organized in Colorado in 1944, and throughout the long consideration of the project, the district board of directors had been active in pursuing the project's construction. Victor A. Paulek, chairman of the board of directors, expressed the opinion that the project had the unanimous support of the people in the area, who were extremely anxious to engage in repayment contracts any time after the project was authorized.[2]

The local commitment thus emanated from the long-standing desire for the very great benefits which it was believed the project would contribute. In answering his own question—Why do people stay with the soil, and suffer hardships caused by poor crops which is due to lack of enough moisture?—Mr. Paulek of the La Plata Conservancy District said:

> They see the water flowing down the rivers from the snow melting high in the mountains and have hopes of getting a project, such as the Animas–La Plata project constructed which would make it possible to apply the water to the excellent loam soil and produce sufficient crops to make an adequate living. . . . Our fathers before us have sought for projects to stabilize the flow of the river. We are still living in faith that sufficient water can come to this area so that our children, and our children's children can have some of the advantages we have missed.[3]

And, in expressing the feelings of the people of Durango, Fred Kroeger told the House subcommittee:

> Periodically we have experienced the heartache, the discouragement and the great economic losses that accrue to a community when the river flows dwindle, when rains do not come, and assets must be liquidated. The benefits to the city of Durango will include those which shall be realized by an agricultural and industrial economy having a dependable long-range supply of water.[4]

The La Plata River had been apportioned in 1925 between New Mexico and Colorado by an interstate compact. However, the insufficient supply in the river had left both states chronically short. Although most of the benefits of the project were to go to Colorado, agricultural interests in northwestern New Mexico also felt a stake. Indeed, in 1964 a petition in support of the project had been signed by 2,324 residents of San Juan County, New Mexico, and a delegation of forty or so had presented it to the governor. Speaking for the La Plata Conservancy District in New Mexico during the 1966 hearings, F. F. Montoya told the House subcommittee,

"Although I have mentioned many problems, there is only one real problem we face, and that is an assured, continuing water supply throughout the growing season. The Animas–La Plata project will do this and automatically solve the problems that I have already discussed."[5]

The Southern Ute Indians and the Ute Mountain Ute Indian tribes desired the Animas–La Plata Project as much as the other residents in the area of the two states where the project was to be located. Chief Jack Horse of the Ute Mountain Ute Tribe told the House subcommittee:

> My tribe has had a feasibility study done of the Fort Lewis Mesa area of the Animas–La Plata project and it showed that lack of water is the only thing that is keeping the tribe from developing a tribal herd of cattle on these lands. Such a herd of cattle would certainly be of benefit to my people. Also, we are very strongly interested in the recreation and other benefits that the tribe can have by use of the Meadows Reservoir of the Animas–La Plata project.

The chief concluded his testimony, "Our good friend Congressman Aspinall has always helped us on any project that we have asked and we feel sure that he will do all in his power again to help us get the water that means so much to us."[6]

Backed by this extremely wide-based popular support, moreover, local advocates of the project had managed to generate such discussion and consideration of the project that by the time the Colorado River Basin Act came up, Animas–La Plata was already quite far along in the series of studies and reviews which precede congressional action. The project had been included among twenty-five potential projects in the Upper Colorado Storage Project Act of 1956 that had been given priority in the completion of planning reports. The local Durango office of the Bureau of Reclamation had worked on a report as time and funds permitted. Preparations had been completed in February 1962 and the district office of the bureau in Salt Lake City had transmitted to the commissioner of reclamation the study and recommendation of feasibility.

The report had recommended that a multipurpose storage and diversion project be constructed in the Animas and La Plata basins. Irrigation benefits were to be primary, including some nonreimbursable benefits to Indian lands belonging to the Southern Ute and Ute Mountain tribes. Some municipal water was to be provided to the city of Durango, Colorado, releasing supplies from irrigation uses in the Florida project area east of the Animas River. Some recreation, fish, and wildlife benefits were also anticipated. The project had been determined by the economic analysis of the Bureau of Reclamation to have an overall benefit/cost ratio of 1.89 to 1. On the basis of direct benefits only, however, the ratio was below unity, .97 to 1.[7]

In accordance with established procedure, a copy of the report had been circulated to a number of relevant departments and agencies before being sent to the president and his staff arm, the Bureau of the Budget, for clearance. Among these were the Bureau of Sports, Fisheries, and Wildlife, the National Park Service, the Forest Service, the Bureau of Mines, the Bureau of Indian Affairs, the Army Corps of Engineers, the Department of Agriculture, and the Public Health Service. Although various comments and suggestions had been made, all of these agencies had indicated that they either supported the project or had no objection to it.[8] Basin states and various state departments had been asked for comments. Both Colorado and New Mexico endorsed the project through their respective water agencies. Among the other states, only California really objected to the project. It did not mention the project specifically in its comments, but offered general reservations about the water supply situation in the whole Colorado River basin and expressed a wish that until there was a determined supply, no new projects should be authorized.[9]

As a part of the process preceding congressional action, the feasibility report proved most important. Its accomplishment can be traced back, moreover, to the assistance given to the local offices of the Bureau of Reclamation in Durango and Grand Junction by the states and localities which were to benefit from the project. In reporting the feasibility study to the secretary of the interior, Commissioner of Reclamation Floyd Dominy had thus stated, "The states of Colorado and New Mexico, the city of Durango and local interests have all actively supported development of the project and have contributed funds toward the cost of project investigations."[10] Water agencies in Colorado had been particularly energetic in pushing the project. The director of the Colorado Water Conservation Board, Felix Sparks, had commented in approving the feasibility study, "We have closely followed the progress of the project investigation since its inception. We are extremely pleased with both the rapidity and thoroughness which have gone into the now completed project report."[11]

As already mentioned, part of the local support for the project came from New Mexico, and the state had approved the feasibility report. However, relative to Colorado, the state had far fewer benefits to anticipate, and there were certain risks involved to New Mexico in an interstate project where she was decidedly the junior partner. But because New Mexico is central to this study, the perspective of New Mexico on Animas–La Plata must become the subject of particularly close scrutiny.

The interest and influence of New Mexico in the Animas–La Plata Project were focused mainly in the person of State Engineer S. E. Reynolds, the chief officer in the state for water matters. Since part of the benefits of the project were to accrue to New Mexico and since the project was to use substantially the remainder of New Mexico's upper basin entitlement, this principal spokesman for New Mexico in water affairs, aside from Senator Clinton P. Anderson, had a real stake in the disposition of the project proposal.

The state engineer in New Mexico has the job of general supervision of the waters of the state and their appropriation, measurement, and distribution. In his role as secretary of the Interstate Stream Commission, he is also involved in interstate negotiation and congressional action related to the conservation and development of water in the state. The state engineer is appointed by and is responsible to the governor. In practice, however, the tenure of the post is relatively secure, and Mr. Reynolds had served for nearly fourteen years under both Republican and Democratic governors. All of the interstate stream commissioners are appointed by the governor, and all but the state engineer represent major irrigation districts or sections of the state.[12] The position of the state engineer, then, puts the man who occupies it in touch with local sentiment in water matters and, at the same time, involves him with the protection of the water interests of the whole state. As further evidence of Reynolds's power base, he continued to serve in the same capacity for more than twenty years after the period of this case study.

Mr. Reynolds was both aware of the support of local people and cognizant of larger concerns in relation to the Animas–La Plata Project. I. J. Courey, resident of the northwestern section of New Mexico, chairman of the Interstate Stream Commission, and member of the La Plata Conservancy District, strongly expressed his locality's desire for a steady water supply. In response, the state and its engineer were more than willing to go along with the project. At the same time, it was expected that Colorado, with its powerful congressman Wayne Aspinall, would provide whatever push could be supplied to move the project along. Consequently, the state engineer saw his role to be that of maximizing the project's benefits to New Mexico.[13]

One of New Mexico's concerns was water supply. This project was to use up the remainder of the 11 percent of upper basin water apportioned to New Mexico. As the last upper basin project, Animas–La Plata competed with all other possible projects. It also threatened some present water uses, especially if the supply of water should turn out to be less than that required for the project.

Another of New Mexico's concerns was the operation of the project. It was important that New Mexico water users be treated equitably. A compact dividing the water in the La Plata basin had existed since 1929, but relations had not always been completely peaceful. For example, in his *Report* for the years 1964 to 1966, the state engineer had said:

> During September 1963, Colorado on two occasions diverted all waters of La Plata River without approval required by Article II, paragraph 3 of the compact. New Mexico protested these unilateral actions to officials of the State of Colorado, and requested assurance that such actions would not recur.[14]

New Mexico was particularly bothered by the interpretation given by Colorado to Article 9 of the Upper Colorado River Compact in regard to the operation of Navajo Dam in the San Juan–Chama project. If this same interpretation were given to Animas–La Plata, New Mexico water users would not get treatment equal with Colorado users. The state engineer felt assurances were necessary.[15]

Repayment of the project also concerned New Mexico. The project was to be heavily subsidized by the Upper Colorado River Basin Fund in which both New Mexico and Colorado had an account. Reimbursement for some benefits was to come from taxes and charges levied in both states. Mr. Reynolds had an interest in seeing that the financial burden carried by New Mexico was equitable.

Thus, New Mexico's backing of the project was necessarily tempered with caution. The state had benefits to gain from the project and wanted to see it authorized. At the same time, there were interests that needed protection in the authorization process.

The Core Activist and His Perceptions

The most prominent political figure who was in the position of being sensitive to the extent of local support for the Animas–La Plata Project and who, at the same time, had the power resources to effect the authorization process was Congressman Wayne Aspinall. Inherently the project had many characteristics to attract the interest and to stimulate the efforts of the chairman of the House Interior and Insular Affairs Committee. And the entrance of a Colorado River basin bill on the legislative scene singularly increased Aspinall's perceptions of gains to be achieved by the authorization of the Animas–La Plata Project.

Congressman Aspinall had, throughout his career, worked with the water interests of Colorado and particularly those of his western slope district. Scattered throughout his constituency and the state were water development projects built under federal auspices for which he could claim a large responsibility. Coloradans had come to expect Congressman Aspinall to exert his influence to locate water projects in the state when and where they wanted them. The Animas–La Plata Project was vigorously desired, moreover, by the local water users who were the backbone of Aspinall's political support at home.

In addition to its political implication, Animas–La Plata was the sort of water development project in which Congressman Aspinall believed most strongly. It was a reclamation project, the principal benefits of which were irrigation, and it had always been the chairman's view that a dollar spent on reclamation was never wasted. Even if the nation had become 70 percent urban, people in cities must eat, food must be produced, and water must be available to produce food. The reclamation dollar keeps on producing for the nation long after it has been paid back by water users and the project has paid out. Development of undeveloped lands, according to Congressman Aspinall, is a good investment.[16]

It was a part of Aspinall's credo as chairman of the House Interior and Insular Affairs Committee that projects endorsed by his committee should meet all the regularly established criteria and be dealt with through orderly procedures. The Animas–La Plata Project had the virtue of having successfully passed a number of tests. It had been reported as feasible by the Bureau of Reclamation. It had the endorsement of the state water agency in Colorado, the Colorado Water Conservation Board, and its director, Felix Sparks. It had a benefit/cost ratio, although not impressive, greater than unity when indirect benefits were taken into account. And, it had the most important advantage of being well within Colorado's entitlement to water under the Upper Basin Compact which had given Colorado 51 percent of the water above Lees Ferry.

The prospect of the passage of the Central Arizona Project raised the specter of water shortage for Colorado which would cut into the state's basic entitlement. Indeed, water supply, a hydrological question, would become one of the most hotly debated political questions in the passage of the Colorado River Basin Act. Joining the debate, Chairman Aspinall expressed doubt that there was sufficient water in the river to make the CAP feasible without employing water to which upper basin states were entitled. He voiced this concern in a May 21, 1965, letter to all the basin state governors asking their estimates of water in the Colorado River. In line with the lower basin agreements operative at this time, Arizona, Nevada, and California coordinated a response, August 13, 1965, which stated that probabilities were that substantial reserves in mainstream storage would tide the basin over during the period between the time when the CAP became operative and when the importation works were constructed.[17] Congressmen Rhodes and Udall responded personally in a letter to the chairman expressing the hope that the basin states would not be caught up in a numbers game on Colorado River water. They noted that the assessment of available water depended very much upon the period within the recorded history of river flow chosen for analysis.[18] Arizonans preferred the unusually wet period from 1906 to 1959, from which the largest supply could be projected.

Rather than being reassured, Chairman Aspinall's misgivings about the risks taken by Colorado in the authorization of the CAP were further reinforced by a study done for the Upper Colorado River Basin Commission by the Denver firm of Tipton and Kalmbach.[19] Its findings indicated that there was not enough water in the basin to supply both entitlements and the Mexican treaty burden. Royce Tipton concluded from the analysis:

It would appear extremely unwise to authorize the construction of a project in the lower basin on the supposition that there will be enough unused water in the upper basin to supply the needs of the project until importation of water is made. If the Central Arizona Project is to be authorized, the authorization for the importation of water into the Colorado River Basin should be made at the same time.[20]

Provided Aspinall's fears and the Tipton report were correct, the Central Arizona Project could not be operated without borrowing the unused water flowing down the river to which the upper basin was entitled. Chairman Aspinall suspected that once Arizona put Colorado's water to use, it would not be possible to reclaim it. Judging from the behavior of California which was using more than her entitlement and yet which regularly failed to back water development projects in other states in the basin on the basis of supply shortages, the chairman could not rationally anticipate the support of Arizona for upstream projects which would take away water it was already using.

So Congressman Aspinall reacted to the supply shortage threat by seeking to insure Colorado's fair share of water. One kind of insurance was a firm plan to import water from outside the basin to make the river whole. Consequently, the chairman supported, along with other upper basin states and California, studies to bring water to the Southwest from the Columbia. He also desired the Grand Canyon dams which would produce funds to make importation financially possible.

Another kind of insurance, one which would provide a backstop for Colorado if importation did not materialize, was to authorize projects which would use up the remainder of Colorado's water rights in the upper basin. And offering this insurance were such projects as Animas–La Plata and four others on the western slope: the West Divide, Dallas Creek, Dolores, and the San Miguel. In the process of being prepared for presentation to Congress, these projects would, if constructed, allow the state to use up all of its water. The chairman thereby determined to have these projects authorized at the same time as the CAP.

The Chairman of the House Interior and Insular Affairs Committee, moreover, had a great deal of leverage with which to make good on his demands. He had all the tools recounted in the previous chapter with which to block legislation others wanted unless they went along with the chairman, and he could use his influence positively to push the projects through the legislative maze. In addition, these projects had certain inherent advantages in the legislative process which increased Chairman Aspinall's influence. Their construction threatened no basic interests of persons or groups influential in authorization. New Mexico was implicated and her interests in Animas–La Plata were different from those of Colorado, but she nevertheless favored the project. No other state was really involved even if California had raised her usual question about shortages in the basin in reviewing the feasibility report. Nor could Colorado's demands be judged unreasonable. Other states were demanding guarantees and projects as the price of support for the CAP. California had in 1965 managed to obtain, along with other favors, a 4.4 guarantee from the Arizonans. Nevada had got Arizona's support for the Southern Nevada Supply Project. In demanding the five Colorado projects, then, Aspinall was simply following suit. Further, the seven-state agreement was in the process of being formulated at this time, and there were strong pressures upon political actors within the basin to be accommodating and agreeable. These were all factors Chairman Aspinall would manipulate.

The Process of Building Consent

Core activist Aspinall, as might be expected given the foregoing factors, made the strategic move which injected the drama into this case of reclamation politics as usual once the 89th Congress got underway in 1966. He let it be known that any Colorado River basin bill reported by his committee would have to include the five Colorado projects next in line for authorization. Among its other consequences, his action wrenched Animas–La Plata and the other projects out of the slow routine of study and clearance. It also threw those with a stake in a Colorado River basin bill into frenzy. The political problem was clear to the backers of a basin bill. Chairman Aspinall had somehow to be satisfied and the five projects readied for congressional consideration.

But this task was not to prove easy, for the proposition of putting the Animas–La Plata Project into the bill had been rendered tremendously more difficult by an action which had just been taken by the Bureau of the Budget. After holding the project from April 10, 1964, it rejected the proposal on February 11, 1966.[21] To understand this action it is necessary to look at Animas–La Plata from the perspective of the Budget Bureau rather than from the viewpoints of its various locally based backers.

Unlike the major activists in favor of the project, the Bureau of the Budget had no reason to be receptive to the local irrigation interests backing the project. Its main constituency is the president, and the Budget Bureau (and its successor the Office of Management and Budget) shares many of the biases of the president, including that of a national constituency. According to Chairman Aspinall, the Budget Bureau is oriented toward social programs and urban areas. Problems of poverty and education are viewed as more salient than the development of undeveloped lands for cultivation.[22] The Budget Bureau encounters an array of programs coming up from the administration to the office of the president for approval as consistent with the president's program. The Budget Bureau's job is to apply certain criteria to sift out the expendable proposals. Benefit/cost analysis provides a convenient tool to accomplish this task. In the view of some persons involved in preparing reclamation proposals for budget clearance, the Bureau of the Budget wields its tool heavy-handedly and often indiscriminately on reclamation projects for which it has little sensitivity. It turns down projects simply on account of their low benefit/cost ratio on paper without taking into account the social benefits not reflected in numbers.[23] Without the indirect benefits which the Budget Bureau objected to including, the benefit/cost ratio of Animas–La Plata was below unity.[24]

And in further reviewing the project, the bureau discovered a number of other characteristics which were undesirable from its point of view. First, the project depended heavily upon subsidies from the Upper Colorado River Basin Fund power revenues with users repaying only a small percentage of the cost. Second, the per-acre cost of the project and the investment per farm were very high.[25] This was partly due to the irrigation planned for Indian land at the edges of the project. The return from irrigation of these Indian lands was expected to be poor while the investment required was very high. As in all Indian irrigation projects, the costs were to be nonreimbursable and borne by the federal government. Third, very little municipal and industrial water, which provides a greater return for the investment, was planned for the project. Consequently, the Bureau of the Budget refused to clear the Animas–La Plata Project.[26]

Among the interests concerned, the Bureau of Reclamation found itself put in a particularly difficult position by the Budget Bureau rejection. The Bureau of Reclamation had a stake in the maintenance of good relations with local interests and the successful clearance of the project it had planned in conjunction with local interests. Of course, since Reclamation was to build and operate the project, it had a further stake in seeing the successful conclusion of the authorization process.

The Bureau of Reclamation found its position on Animas–La Plata made more compelling, however, by the place which the project was made to occupy by Chairman Aspinall in relation to a Colorado River basin bill. The bureau was therein provided with a stronger and more immediate association with the project. The success of this and other projects in Chairman Aspinall's district became important to Reclamation's whole plan of development for the Southwest. The bureau was strongly committed to the CAP and to the Grand Canyon dams. It was in the interest of the Bureau of Reclamation to do all it could to smooth the way for the Colorado projects, if this was the sweetener Chairman Aspinall require to swallow the Arizona project.

For the Reclamation Bureau, the challenge of the chairman was made especially clear in relation to the Animas–La Plata Project. The chairman said that he did not intend to resume hearings on the Central Arizona Project until the difficulty about Budget Bureau approval of Animas–La Plata was cleared up.[27] Congressman Aspinall, moreover, received firm support from his constituency for his stand. In an editorial, the Grand Junction *Daily Sentinel* lauded Mr. Aspinall:

No one in Colorado (and certainly no one in Western Colorado) should fail to praise Congressman Aspinall's courageous stand. Now it is doubtful that the Arizona project will even get a hearing until the Colorado plans, long a part of the Upper Colorado Project, are approved according to agreement.

All this demonstrates once again just how valuable to Colorado is Wayne N. Aspinall. If the Upper Colorado Basin states did not have a man of his stature fighting their battles it would take less than five years for all of the water in Colorado to be stolen, divided and appropriated by Southern California. Reclamation in the Upper Basin states would be left completely and literally high and dry.[28]

For the Reclamation Bureau, the challenge was also clear in relation to the other Colorado projects. All of these projects, except the Dolores, were either months or years away from being ready, under ordinary timing.[29] A top Interior Department source told the Grand Junction *Daily Sentinel* that Secretary Udall had ordered the Bureau of Reclamation to go on overtime, if necessary, to get the reports completed as soon as possible on the San Miguel, Dallas Creek, and West Divide projects. The bureau was, in addition, to revise the Animas–La Plata Project.[30]

A number of bureau officials from Washington, the region, and the locality subsequently met in Denver to rework this latter project. The basic revision to increase economic feasibility was to drop some of the marginal lands from the irrigation service area and to increase the amount of water that would be made available for municipal and industrial uses. One such new demand for municipal water was developed in the city of Farmington, New Mexico. Evidently, the city government was approached by the Bureau of Reclamation to locate some of the Animas–La Plata water there. According to Mayor Floyd G. Davis of Farmington:

The feasibility of the Animas–La Plata Project was in jeopardy without the participation of Farmington and Kirtland Valleys in their use of municipal and industrial water. We were approached by the Bureau of Reclamation and later "politicked" by our good farmer force in the La Plata Valley for an agreement to purchase 15,000 acre feet of water out of a lake to be built just above Farmington. Although Farmington has between 25,000 and 30,000 acre feet of water rights, of which we are only using 5–6,000, we did feel that there was a distinct possibility that here, in the next ten years, some industry could be obtained on the basis of this water, and so we testified in favor of the Animas–La Plata Project and assured them that we would seriously consider the purchase of 15,000 acre feet at the time it became available.

Another possible location for industrial water was the development of coal reserves on Indian lands. Sometime in 1964, the Southern Ute Indian tribe had entered into an agreement with the Peabody Coal Company for the future development of coal resources on the reservation. The coal was to be used in a coal-fueled power plant. The company had later contacted the Bureau of Reclamation concerning the availability of water. As a result, the modified plan of the Animas–La Plata Project decreased the full-service irrigated acreage from 58,900 acres to 46,520 acres and increased the proposed municipal and industrial water from 9,200 acre-feet to 76,200 acre-feet annually. A potential dam and reservoir was added as a storage facility for the water to be used in the power plant. Most of the marginal irrigated land removed from the project proposal belonged to the Indians. At the same time, this deprivation was made up for by the anticipated benefits of the coal development. As an overall result from the revision, the benefit/cost ratio of the direct benefits was increased from 0.97 to 1, to 1.11 to 1.[32]

Even with a report for a more economically justified project, there was still the pressure of time. Felix Sparks, the director of the Colorado Water Conservation Board, commented on the difficulties. With only a month to go before it was hoped that hearings could begin on the Colorado River Basin Act, there remained much processing to be done on the Animas–La Plata Project, processing which ordinarily consumed years. Usually, from the time feasibility reports are submitted to the secretary, Sparks said, there is a period of six months before such reports go to the president. After the project report is transmitted to the president, it is then reviewed by the Budget Bureau, this review usually taking a period from six months to a year.[33] The problem was to telescope all this time into a few weeks.

The time before the secretary's transmittal to the president was compressed by facilitating the review by the states and by other federal agencies. The seven-state agreement then existing streamlined state approval. California, which had previously opposed the project on the basis of supply, simply sent a telegram saying it did not oppose the project.[34] The Army Corps of Engineers, after first balking by maintaining it would need the full ninety-day review period, ended up by sending a short note saying there were no objections.[35]

The Bureau of the Budget as well as Reclamation began to feel the heat. There was a great deal of political pressure from the basin states, from within the Interior Department, and from the Congress upon the Bureau of the Budget to act positively and quickly on the Colorado projects. The Budget Bureau accommodated these pressures by acting quickly and met them halfway by not objecting to any of the five Colorado projects even though it did not approve them. The secretary of the interior received replies on the reports submitted April 6 and 13 in a letter dated April 30, 1966. As an overall comment, the Budget Bureau said of the five projects:

Since these new projects in the Upper Colorado Basin would require such heavy subsidies for irrigation farmers, we question the desirability in areas of critically short water supply of Federal Government sponsorship without further consideration of both alternative uses and of supplemental water sources.

Of the Animas–La Plata Project, the Budget Bureau said:

The revised Animas–La Plata project would also have a heavy dependence on power revenues, with a water users' repayment of only 13.1 percent. The investment per farm would be about $157,000. The project has a cost per acre of $840 and a low direct benefit-cost ratio (1.1:1). While there appears to be no immediate need for the 23,500 acre feet of municipal and industrial water that would be delivered to the Ute Mountain Tribe Reservation, the allocation of this water for these purposes rather than irrigation improves the project. The charge for municipal industrial water seems very low considering that it will probably be used in large part for developing a profitable coal-steam power industry.[36]

The Bureau of the Budget report concluded with a carefully worded statement which did not approve the projects but which was not, at the same time, the kind of rejection which would have prevented the Department of the Interior from referring the projects to Congress for authorization:

In summary, for the reasons expressed above, the Bureau of the Budget would favor deferral of at least the West Divide, San Miguel and Dallas Creek projects at this time, pending the establishment of the National Water Commission and completion of its review of related water problems. We believe that this course of action will permit water developments needed at this time in the Colorado Basin to proceed, but at the same time provide a basis for thorough consideration of the fundamental issues involved and a recommended program that will be in the best interests of the people of the Upper and Lower Colorado Basin, as well as the Nation as a whole.[37]

New Mexico's Concurrence

In the course of all the pressure to revise the Animas–La Plata Project, complete feasibility reports on three other projects, and get all five cleared by the basin states and related federal agencies, the concerns of New Mexico about the Animas–La Plata Project were quickly disposed of. One issue was taken care of even before the crash program to get the five projects in the bill had begun. That was the matter of the sufficiency of New Mexico's allotment of water to meet the demands of the project. This was really an issue between the Bureau of Reclamation and New Mexico. The bureau precipitated New Mexico's concern about supply by refusing to issue long-term contracts for water from Navajo Reservoir for municipal and industrial uses until it was convinced of the sufficiency of New Mexico's water supply. The New Mexico Interstate Stream Commission hesitated to commit large amounts of water to irrigation purposes in the Animas–La Plata Project until it was certain that there was enough water to fill the municipal and industrial demand. The commission acted to defer its position on Animas–La Plata and recommended to the governor that he ask Senator Anderson to request the secretary of the interior to make a determination of New Mexico's supplies. In January of 1964, the secretary released a finding that the state had enough water with Animas–La Plata to serve anticipated municipal and industrial demands for at least forty years from 1965. State Engineer Reynolds accepted this finding, and New Mexico agreed to support the project. As a safeguard, however, Mr. Reynolds stipulated that the state might reopen the secretary's finding if the year 2005 were approaching and the state needed more water.[38]

Another of New Mexico's fears related to the operation of the project. Under a certain interpretation given to Article 9 of the Upper Colorado River Basin Compact, New Mexico users might suffer shortages caused by junior appropriations in Colorado. It was not sufficient reassurance for New Mexico that the Department of the Interior was to operate the project at all times[39] or that Colorado agreed not to interpret Article 9 in a way prejudicial to New Mexico. New Mexico's position was that only a compact between New Mexico and Colorado stating operating principles, ratified by both states, and written into the authorizing legislation was sufficient protection.[40]

There are indications that Colorado balked for a time at the notion of such a formal commitment. But by the time of the hearings in May of 1966, Mr. Reynolds could testify to the House subcommittee:

I am pleased to report that, while we have not yet settled on specific language for the Animas–La Plata Project Compact we are in substantial agreement in principle and there appears to be no reason why the compact cannot be executed and ratified in time to avoid any delay in project construction.

The negotiations on the terms of the compact, conducted between Mr. Reynolds and Mr. Sparks, were successfully completed,[41] and New Mexico achieved her goal of firm legal assurances on operation of the project.

Another issue between New Mexico and Colorado also remained unsettled on the eve of the hearings. This was the matter of an ad valorem tax which was required under the upper basin fund of cities benefiting indirectly from the project and which under the arrangement of conservancy districts in Colorado was to be applied to the cities, such as Durango, that were to profit from Animas–La Plata. Under the bureau's plan, the boundaries of the La Plata Conservancy District in New Mexico were to be extended so that the cities of Farmington and Aztec could be included for taxing purposes. The New Mexico cities objected, and Mr. Reynolds suggested that power revenues credited to New Mexico in the upper basin fund be substituted for the amount of the taxes. Chairman Aspinall was not certain that this was an equitable solution if Colorado cities were required to assume burdens from which New Mexico cities would be immune. Mr. Reynolds distinguished the situations by maintaining that Colorado cities were within the irrigation area, while New Mexico cities were not, the latter only becoming involved because they were willing to contract for municipal water for which they would pay a fair price.[42]

Settlement on this issue, however, was not necessary to proceed with authorization of the project, and Chairman Aspinall did not seem anxious to press the issue to a conclusion.[43] Mr. Reynolds simply requested that the Bureau of Reclamation give further consideration to alternatives for changing the boundaries of the La Plata Conservancy District. The final settlement was to be negotiated in time among various participants, including the La Plata Conservancy District, the bureau, and the cities involved.[44]

Legislative History of the Project

Even though the 1966 bill failed to get to the floor of the House, once the five Colorado projects were included in the 1966 bill there was little question that they would remain a part of any package that could successfully negotiate the legislative hurdles. The position of Congressman Aspinall made this a certainty. It was only a matter of how the projects would be included, what form they would take, and what support for the whole bill would be forthcoming from their inclusion.

1967 action by the 90th Congress began in the Senate. The administration in its presentation before the Senate Committee enunciated the position of the Bureau of the Budget on the five projects, recommending deferral of at least three. When pressed on the issue, however, Secretary Udall made it clear that the administration would not offer any serious objections if all five of the projects were included.[45] During the markup of the bill, Senator Hayden introduced an amendment adding to the bill the five Colorado projects, which he and Senator Jackson were sponsoring. This was a move to soften the position of Senator Gordon Allott, Republican from Colorado, as well as a recognition of the political imperatives in the House. In addition, including the five projects accommodated Senator Anderson who was insisting upon the Animas–La Plata Project in the bill.[46]

Yet the inclusion of the five Colorado projects did very little to placate Colorado's senior senator, who remained adamantly opposed to any bill which did not also include an importation study and the Grand Canyon dams. He called the five projects a "political sop" and charged that, because of the water shortage the CAP would create without compensating augmentation, the bill would severely hinder future development in the upper Colorado River basin.[47] He doubted that the five projects would ever be built because of lack of funds and water. One of the reasons why Senator Allott was not appeased might have been the location of all five of the projects on the western slope. Allott's constituency was statewide, and most of Colorado's population is located in the cities on the eastern slope. For Senator Allott's larger electorate, the five projects did not represent the sort of reward they did for Aspinall's district.

Throughout 1967, Congressman Aspinall held out against reporting a Colorado River basin bill from his committee. Any bill, he said, had to bring in some kind of augmentation study to see to it that the Colorado River got enough water. The dearth of such provisions in the Senate bill killed the legislation for the session. Later, when pressure was brought on him from the Arizonans to move the bill, including a letter sent from Senator Hayden to newspapers in Aspinall's district, the congressman responded bitterly. He called the CAP bill a half-baked proposition and accused the Arizonans of deliberately dividing the upper basin states and his own district by putting the five Colorado projects into the bill. This had infuriated the other upper basin states, he complained, and had caused him difficulties in his district. "Whether I return to Congress is of very little importance to me," he maintained. "It will never be said of me, 'he sold out'." [48]

In the fall of 1967, a number of meetings were held between Congressman Aspinall, Felix Sparks, and various members of the Arizona task force and congressional delegation to settle upon the sort of guarantees of upper basin entitlements which would give sufficient comfort to the Interior Committee chairman. At this point, the notion of concurrent construction of the five Colorado projects with the CAP emerged. Congressman Aspinall wanted to state in the legislation that the five projects and the CAP would begin to operate at the same time. In such event, there would be no question of Arizona's using water rightfully belonging to Colorado. This concept implied concurrent funding of the five Colorado projects along with the Central Arizona Project. Such a commitment grated against the sensitivities of Congressman Rhodes, who took pride in the independence of the Public Works Subcommittee of the House Appropriations Committee to make its own judgments. [49] In the end, however, the Arizonans accepted the concurrent construction provision in the bill. This was one of the components of the situation which prompted Congressman Aspinall to act on the CAP bill early in the second session of the 90th Congress.

The story of the majority building successfully completed on the basin bill in 1968 was told in chapter 4. Despite the concurrent construction language, Senator Allott continued to express strong misgivings about the bill. His position was a minority one on the Senate committee and in the conference, however, reducing the senator to oratory rather than effective action. He did put the Arizonans on notice that he took the idea of concurrent funding of the Colorado projects seriously.[50] As the historical update in chapter 9 attests, Senator Allott was appropriately skeptical.

Overview

The authorization of the Animas–La Plata Project in the Colorado River Basin Act and the part which New Mexico played in it are very minor events when compared with the Central Arizona Project. At the same time, the pattern of politics on this project is just as illustrative of reclamation politics as that through which the largest reclamation project of all became law. And it is a good bit more characteristic of the low-key way most projects are passed.

Typically the genesis of the project and the moving force behind it came from the locality. Local activity had pushed the project to a place where Congressman Aspinall could pick up the proposal and propel it through the legislative process. The history of Animas–La Plata illustrates the importance to the success of a project of a link with a political figure who senses a stake in it and possesses the political influence to reflect his stake effectively. The power and perspective of Chairman Aspinall tells considerably more about why Animas–La Plata was authorized than the feasibility reports prepared by the Bureau of Reclamation.

The story of Animas–La Plata puts some of the hurdles and tests presented to projects in the course of authorization in a political framework. Benefit/cost analysis as applied by the Bureau of the Budget did not restructure the project or change the basic plan. It simply prompted the activists to add on some new municipal and industrial features for which there was little immediate demand. The periods of clearance and review, designed to subject every project to close technical scrutiny, were, like the benefit/cost analysis, adjusted to the imperatives of political power. It should be noted that once the five Colorado projects were successfully reported to Congress, the Bureau of the Budget lost whatever influence it had over the sort of projects authorized.

The Animas–La Plata Project also presents some insights into the application of political leverage and the importance of timing. Congressman Aspinall was successful in attaching his five Colorado projects onto the Central Arizona Project because the Arizona activists were committed to getting a CAP. They were in a hurry and were not willing to take the time and effort, and above all the risk, which would have been required to overrun the chairman on this matter. Congressman Aspinall's leverage here was negative. Accepting the five projects partially removed a block in the committee and on the floor, but it added little support for the CAP. In the same way Mr. Reynolds and the New Mexicans exercised some political leverage on the Coloradans. It was certain that Chairman Aspinall wanted the five projects and could provide the political force to get them through. Consequently, in a minor way, the New Mexicans could take advantage of the positive pressure behind the project and the shortage of time. They managed to get an interstate compact and perhaps some other protections from the bill which they might not have gotten if the situation had been different. The political leverage of the New Mexicans was the potential of presenting a bothersome and time-consuming problem. Like the Arizonans who accepted the five projects, the Coloradans were willing to pay the price.

6

Negotiations on the Gila: New Water for New Mexico

Introduction

The story of the Arizona–New Mexico negotiations on the Gila recounts the way activists from New Mexico used political leverage to get water in addition to the state's legal entitlement. This new water for New Mexico clearly came from Arizona. It came out of the supply Arizona anticipated from the Central Arizona Project. In the words of Congressman Morris Udall, "The decision to give away her water to New Mexico was a terribly bitter one for Arizona."[1] Nevertheless, it was one which the Arizona leaders could not help making, given the imperatives of the political situation.

Unlike the Animas–La Plata Project authorized in the Colorado River Basin Act, the acquisition of new water on the Gila for New Mexico probably would not have come to fruition outside that particular context. The justifications in legal terms and the feasibility in engineering terms were not sufficiently compelling to provide a firm basis for New Mexico's claim. Attempts were made to build a case for additional water on these grounds, but the persuasiveness of the arguments never matched the sheer political power which New Mexico wielded.

Genesis of the Issue

The seed of controversy between Arizona and New Mexico was sown in the Supreme Court case, *Arizona v. California* (1964). New Mexico was brought into the case against her will, and in the course of litigation, an apportionment was made of the waters of the Gila between Arizona and New Mexico. The result was less water than New Mexico requested of the Court and hoped to acquire. The Colorado River Basin Act presented New Mexico with an opportunity to recoup.

The Gila is an interstate stream which arises in high, timbered terrain in southwestern New Mexico and flows to meet the Colorado River in Arizona. Arizona's water rights on the Gila and those of Indian tribes in Arizona are old and well established. Most New Mexico uses upstream are subsequent in time and junior to the downstream appropriations. In the case of *Arizona v. California*, New Mexico sought to establish a firm entitlement to present uses on the Gila. She further claimed water for future development. During the hearings, New Mexicans tried to show that if a system of storage facilities were built on the Gila, New Mexico could increase her uses without jeopardizing downstream users.

The special master appointed by the Court to hear the case accepted New Mexico's contention as far as present uses were concerned. As to additional water for New Mexico for future development, the special master's report stated, "It is here, however, that priority of appropriation has its greatest effect. It would be unreasonable in the extreme to reserve water for future use in New Mexico when senior downstream appropriators in Arizona remain unsatisfied." [2] The master went on to state that he could not formulate his judgments on the basis of the effects of possible future water development projects on the Gila. This would be to formulate his decree on hypothetical facts. If conditions changed, the master said, the decree could be changed.

Once New Mexico's entitlement was limited to present uses, she was put in the position of having to prove their extent. Evidence had to be quickly prepared, and the representatives of the state felt that the pressure of time prevented the accumulation and presentation of the best case for New Mexico. Perhaps as a consequence, the master found many of New Mexico's claims for present uses unconvincing. The very limited amount of water and irrigated acreage recognized in the master's report was a great disappointment to the state, and her representatives requested a chance to provide additional evidence.

In lieu of a rehearing, attorneys and engineers representing New Mexico and Arizona got together with the master and began negotiations on New Mexico's rightful portion of the Gila. A week of meetings finally culminated in a stipulation as to New Mexico's present uses agreed to by both states. The water accorded to New Mexico in the stipulation was greater than that provided by the master, but less than New Mexico's original contention.

The assumptions underlying the stipulated agreement between Arizona and New Mexico have been subject to varying interpretations. New Mexicans were unhappy with the draft report of the special master and felt that the state had improved its position through negotiations with Arizona. As in the case of most compromises, however, New Mexico was not entirely content. She requested and the Court included in the decree Article 9, through which any of the parties to the case could, because of a change in the circumstances, apply for additional relief.[3] Her representatives felt that this language, as well as verbal notice given to Arizona, were ample indications to Arizona that New Mexico viewed the stipulation as temporary and only the best she could manage at the moment.

New Mexicans viewed the introduction of the Central Arizona Project bill as the sort of new circumstance which justified a reexamination of

New Mexico's entitlement on the Gila. Since the CAP could provide additional water for Arizona users of the Gila, New Mexicans believed that New Mexico was acting in good faith, completely consistent with and within the provisions of the *Arizona v. California* decree to demand additional benefits for her citizens on the Gila in conjunction with the CAP.

In contrast, Arizonans felt that New Mexico's acceptance of the stipulation and the recommendation to the special master that it be adopted represented a resignation by New Mexico of any claims to additional water. Arizonans felt that they had been generous in the negotiations and had only concurred in the result because it was assumed that New Mexico would stand by an implicit understanding that the settlement was final and complete.[4]

The Central Activists in the Controversy and Their Perceptions

The position of New Mexico on the division of Gila water was shaped and represented by her state engineer, S. E. Reynolds. Unlike the Animas–La Plata Project where Mr. Reynolds was simply a protector of New Mexico interests, he was a core activist on the Gila question. He was one of the officials of New Mexico water agencies who held the vision of new water on the Gila for New Mexico during the 1950s when New Mexico was brought in as a party to the Supreme Court suit.[5] As a witness before the Court, he contended that the Gila could be developed by a series of reservoirs which would allow New Mexico to greatly increase its supply.

The decree represented a setback to Mr. Reynolds, but he refused to view the situation as hopeless. Subsequent to the decree, he concentrated upon building a case to eventually change the judgment.[6] Under the guidance of Mr. Reynolds, New Mexico provided funds to the Bureau of Reclamation in 1963 to make a reconnaissance investigation of the potentialities for improved and more intensive utilization of the land and water resources in the Gila River basin in New Mexico. The bureau reported that there was an obvious need for area redevelopment on the Gila and that such redevelopment could be advanced and the general economy of the area enhanced and stabilized through a series of land and water development programs.[7] This bureau report provided Mr. Reynolds with part of the record he desired. At the same time, the Arizonans questioned its value since the criteria established by New Mexico instructed the bureau to ignore the water rights downstream in Arizona in determining the feasibility of New Mexican water projects. Arizonans contended that the proposed development could not occur without jeopardizing the senior rights of users in the San Carlos area of Arizona.

Mr. Reynolds made his first direct approach to the Arizonans on October 25, 1962, when a meeting was held which he had requested of the Arizona state engineer, William Gookin. At that time, with members of the New Mexico and Arizona interstate stream commissions present, Mr. Reynolds argued for a negotiated agreement to give New Mexico 30,000 to 40,000 acre-feet more water on the Gila.[8] He maintained that the CAP, as presented by the Arizonans, offered nothing for New Mexico. Although Hooker Dam was included in the bill, it would never be built. The evaporation from the reservoir was anticipated to be between 1,000 and 3,000 acre-feet a year, and since New Mexico already exceeded the allotment of Gila water under the decree, she could not permit the dam to be built and still fulfill her legal obligations.

Mr. Reynolds was disappointed at the reaction of the people in the Arizona water agencies at this meeting and at a subsequent one held March 23, 1963. Arizonans agreed to talk, but refused to negotiate.[9] They said that the matter of Gila water was settled and that there was no basis for New Mexican demands. It was the position of the Arizonans that New Mexico had gotten and was getting substantial benefits from Arizona. Hooker was infeasible and could never be built without the CAP. Under the stipulated agreement, Arizona was giving New Mexico 16 percent more water and 15 percent more irrigated land under present uses than had the special master in his report. Further, Arizonans had supported the Upper Colorado River Storage Project Act and the San Juan–Chama project, both of which benefited New Mexico. In response to these arguments, Mr. Reynolds stated that New Mexico would not support the CAP unless there were a negotiated settlement on the Gila.

The threat made by Mr. Reynolds had real content because of the support provided and the power wielded by another core activist in the Gila controversy, Senator Clinton P. Anderson. Among the senator's long-time goals were to get for New Mexico her full and fair entitlement to water and to see that water put to beneficial use, under federal authorization of water development projects whenever necessary.[10] He had been eminently successful in achieving his aims. The senator played a large role in New Mexico's achievement of federal authorization of a number of water development projects, including the San Juan–Chama project. New Mexico was using all the water to which she was entitled in the lower basin. With the authorization of the Animas–La Plata Project, the state would substantially exhaust its potential supply in the upper basin. In regard to utilization of water, New Mexico was further along than any other state in the basin except California.

Senator Anderson had the power resources to register effectively the commitment he felt to the state in water matters. The senator's salutary career afforded him deference by his constituents, colleagues, and members of the administration. Among his numerous posts in state and national government, he was secretary of agriculture for a time during the Truman administration. He had entered the Senate in 1948 and had subsequently accumulated considerable seniority. During his lengthy tenure, he had distinguished himself in a number of issue areas, including medicine and atomic energy, as well as natural resources. In these fields he came to be regarded by his fellow senators as an expert whose judgment was valuable. The senator had a particular reputation as a specialist in water and as a chief spokesman for the upper Colorado River basin.[11] This expertise was developed and utilized during his tenure as chairman of the Senate Interior and Insular Affairs Committee, a post he vacated to his colleague and friend, Senator Henry Jackson, and in his position as chairman of the Subcommittee on Water and Power.

Senator Anderson's style and skill in the use of influence were among his political assets. Even though his word carried much weight, the senator was not in the habit of speaking out often. He was aware of the value of keeping his own counsel and preserving his influence for use at times when he really wanted to have an impact.[12] Because Senator Anderson was a conservationist about power, he had accumulated a great store of debts and obligations owed him by other senators upon which he could draw. Part of the senator's impact was based solely on his past reputation. Although he had been victim to a stroke and his pace had visibly slowed by the time of the Colorado River Basin Act, associates, remembering the past, displayed a touch of awe. His aloofness and reputation for sudden temper reinforced the inclination of others not to stand in his way.

Senator Anderson's view of the controversy over division of Gila water was that Arizona should be willing to negotiate a settlement affording New Mexico additional water. He frequently relied upon the judgments of State Engineer Reynolds in water matters. He was convinced of the importance to the state of this additional water and of New Mexico's moral and legal right to demand it. In an interview with the *Albuquerque Journal* on February 15, 1964, he had established his stance clearly by stating that he would not support the Pacific Southwest Water Plan which embodied the Central Arizona Project until there was a settlement on the Gila.

Since Arizonans in the Senate were no real competition, Senator Hayden being indisposed and Senator Fannin being far from Anderson's equal, the part of defending Arizona in the Gila affair fell upon the most senior and prestigious Arizona members of the House, Congressmen John Rhodes and Morris Udall. The two were deeply committed to smoothing the way for the CAP and were Arizona's principal activists. Also, the pair had some assets in their access to Senator Anderson. Congressman Rhodes had actively supported the passage of the Colorado River Basin Storage Project Act in 1956, Senator Anderson having been one of the primary backers of that bill. In the course of their common effort, then, Senator Anderson had come to have real respect for Congressman Rhodes. So, too, Senator Anderson liked Morris Udall; these were men with whom he was willing to deal.[13]

The perceptions which the Arizona congressmen had of possible negotiations with New Mexico on the division of the Gila combined conflicting views. One perspective was the feelings of the Arizonans, particularly the people in water agencies. A contrasting perspective came from an examination of the majority-building processes in Congress and an analysis of what it would require to get the CAP through the national legislature.

The people in Arizona water agencies with whom Congressmen Rhodes and Udall worked closely on the CAP felt bitterly betrayed by New Mexico's demand for additional water. The participants in the stipulation negotiations in *Arizona v. California* believed New Mexico had abandoned a solemn agreement.[14] Arizonans felt that their past support of water development in New Mexico should be paid back in kind.

Arizonans were fearful about reopening legal decisions. They looked upon the decision in *Arizona v. California* as a landmark victory. Any change in the decree represented a relinquishment of what had been won. The difficulty which Arizonans had experienced in accepting a 4.4 guarantee to California was evidence of this point of view. Further, Arizonans anticipated that the Globe Equity Decree No. 59 would also have to be upset. This legal settlement was the basis of water rights in both New Mexico and Arizona.

Reexamination of water rights would, moreover, provide an opportunity for all parties disgruntled with present legal entitlements to make new claims. Arizonans looked forward, for example, to the presentation of demands for additional water to be made by the Pima-Maricopa Indians. The settlement of the conflicts precipitated by overturning the Globe case would be tremendously time-consuming. Arizona's adversaries elsewhere in the basin might well use this time to advantage.[15]

There was a possibility that users of Gila water in Arizona would experience real deprivations if New Mexico should withhold more than her allotment under *Arizona v. California*. Irrigators might suffer, and less water would be available for power generation at Coolidge Dam. These misfortunes might eventually be expressed in political discontent which would be troublesome to Arizona politicians.

Looking toward the legislative situation to be encountered by the Central Arizona Project, the Arizona congressmen had, however, to see New Mexico's contentions in quite a different light. Senator Anderson was a crucial power center. He chaired the Subcommittee on Water and Power of the Senate Committee on Interior and Insular Affairs, the committee with jurisdiction over reclamation legislation. This position afforded him sharp implements to carve out the fate of the CAP, including timing, scheduling, and structuring of hearings. Further, the man's tremendous stature in the Senate magnified his influence far beyond that of the ordinary subcommittee chairman. This was reflected in his close relationship with Senator Henry Jackson, chairman of the full Committee on Interior and Insular Affairs, and another critical power center for the Arizonans. It was the conviction of Congressman Udall that Senator Anderson had to be first accommodated before Senator Jackson could be approached.[16] This could only be accomplished through a settlement on Gila water. Balancing the alternatives, the Arizona congressmen felt they had to negotiate. Call it blackmail, as did many Arizonans, the demands had to be met. The only question was how large the price was to be. This was established in the course of the delicate bargaining through which a New Mexico–Arizona agreement was reached.

History of the Negotiations

Up until the spring of 1966, the Arizonans held firm in their position that the division of Gila water had been settled finally in *Arizona v. California*. Congressman Udall articulated Arizona's stance during the testimony of Mr. Reynolds and Mr. Claude Mann, legal advisor to the New Mexico Interstate Stream Commission, presented to the House committee in August and September of 1965. Through a series of pointed questions, the Arizona congressman indicated his belief that New Mexico was being offered real benefits in the Colorado River Basin Act: all the water due New Mexico under the decree and Hooker Dam which would regulate flood flows, provide a more reliable and orderly seasonal supply of water, and give southwestern New Mexico a recreation facility. On the other hand, he argued, Arizona had a great deal to lose by accommodating New Mexico, most importantly, her water. Arizona's legal entitlement on the Colorado would be cut by whatever amount she gave New Mexico. So, maintained Udall, New Mexico should be willing to wait for importation to receive additional water, just as the other basin states had to wait.[17]

Representatives of other basin states at the 1965 hearings afforded the New Mexico position no more sympathy than it received from Arizona. Congressman Craig Hosmer, Republican of California, charged, "In essence, you want to hold the lower basin project for ransom, for some water. . . . You call it equitable apportionment. I call it ransom." He summarized his reaction by saying, "Well, I think you have a real clever scheme here from New Mexico's standpoint, but I am still not convinced about it being equitable in relation to the other states, nor am I convinced that once having gotten this 46,000 acre-feet ransom water that New Mexico could have an incentive to be part of the team."[18]

Congressman Aspinall's perceptions of the New Mexico position were those of an upper basin spokesman. He felt that New Mexico was alienating herself from the upper basin, now that she had put most of her entitlement to use. He could accept the claims of New Mexico on the Gila, but he resented that this was the condition of support. The upper basin was worried about the whole matter of supply, and Aspinall believed that New Mexico should be too.[19]

The adverse reception which New Mexican water leaders Reynolds and Mann received at the House committee hearings in 1965 did not soften their determination in the least. It remained the intention of the state engineer to get new water. As Congressman Udall expressed it, "You feel you have a point of leverage with us now in this situation which you would not wish to give up." Mr. Reynolds responded, "We think we have a duty to the citizens of New Mexico to take advantage of this opportunity to get New Mexico's fair share of the Gila system."[20]

The basinwide accord which began to take form on a version of the Colorado River Basin Act, F.R. 4671 in the spring of 1966, resulted in tremendous pressure for the settlement of outstanding issues, including the division of Gila water between Arizona and New Mexico. By later April, the upper basin states, led by Congressman Aspinall who injected the five Colorado projects into the bill, had joined the lower basin states in support of the bill. This left only New Mexico outside the agreement. And, it was at this point that Arizonans determined to negotiate. The momentum built up behind the bill as a result of basin unity was too valuable to be slowed by this relatively minor matter.

Once Arizona had determined to sacrifice some of her water on the Gila to advance the Central Arizona Project, the decisions about the details of the compromise were, according to Congressman Udall, relatively easy for the Arizonans to make.[21] The guiding rule of the Arizona congressmen in the negotiations which followed was the protection of the rights of present water users on the Gila River in Arizona.[22] And since the purpose of the agreement was to promote the quick authorization of the CAP, the Arizonans were anxious that the settlement avoid further conflict and delay.

On April 25, 1966, Representatives Rhodes and Udall made the crucial move in obtaining an interview with Senator Anderson. Discussion at the meeting established the basis of compromise. First, New Mexico was to get additional water on the Gila when the CAP began operation. Fifteen thousand acre-feet, not counting evaporation, was the figure mentioned at this time. Second, Hooker Dam would be authorized in the legislation. The Arizonans preferred that the size be stipulated as a small dam, 222 feet high with reservoir storage of 98,000 acre-feet. Third, the agreement would provide protection for Gila users in the San Carlos Project in Arizona, including reimbursement for power losses at Coolidge Dam caused by water held back in New Mexico. Fourth, when importation of water into the Colorado River basin as contemplated in the House bill was accomplished, New Mexico could increase its consumptive use on the upper Gila River by an additional 25,000 to 30,000 acre-feet.[23]

After the framework for negotiations was established with Senator Anderson, a series of meetings was held among the Arizona congressmen, members of the Arizona task force, and a group of persons from New Mexico water agencies led by State Engineer S. E. Reynolds. These sessions worked on the details of the accord and a mutually agreeable method of enforcement. The issues discussed included the size of Hooker Dam and provisions for enlargement so New Mexico could retain additional water when importation was accomplished. New Mexico cared that the structure be large enough and capable of being made bigger so that all the water anticipated from the agreement could be put to use in New Mexico. Arizona of course was anxious to limit the size of the dam to protect downstream users. The amount of water to be given to New Mexico when the CAP was built was another area of discussion. Between 15,000 and 20,000 acre-feet was the range considered during these discussions. No real controversy developed over provisions to protect Arizona users, including operations of dams in Arizona and reimbursement for power losses. These matters did not really implicate New Mexico.[24]

Various methods of modifying the *Arizona v. California* decree to give force to an agreement on a new division of Gila water were also discussed. New Mexico wanted firm assurances, preferably airtight legal guarantees, that she was to get the new water she desired. New Mexico representatives looked with favor on an interstate compact. Arizona preferred that the method of enforcement be fairly informal, with both states pledging their good intentions. Arizona negotiators wanted to avoid any commitment to time-consuming, complicated legal processes which might create controversy and hold up the CAP.

The bargaining process did not always proceed smoothly. Strong conflicts developed over some of the issues identified above, and misunderstandings arose on other points. When such clashes developed, Senator Anderson was brought directly into the action by either the New Mexico or the Arizona negotiators. At other times, he remained aloof from the bargaining, although he did, at one point, send a letter to Congressman Udall prodding him to come to an accommodation with Mr. Reynolds.[25] He did not, however, attend any of the meetings. Settlements made between the Arizona congressmen and Mr. Reynolds and his colleagues were referred to the senior senator for ratification.

On May 12, 1966, the Arizona congressmen and Mr. Reynolds agreed upon a set of principles. These were included in a memorandum and sent to Senator Anderson for his consent. The five parts to the settlement were as follows:

1. Hooker Dam shall be constructed to a capacity of 98,000 acre-feet and in such a manner as to permit subsequent enlargement.
2. New Mexico shall be entitled to increase her consumptive use from the Gila by an average of 18,000 acre-feet annually in any period of ten consecutive years, including evaporation. New Mexico shall be further entitled to increase her consumptive use by 30,000 acre-feet annually when works capable of importing 2.55 million acre-feet to the Colorado River system have been completed. The additional consumptive uses shall be subject to all present rights established in the Globe Equity Decree No. 59 and shall be made only to the extent possible without

economic injury or cost to present downstream users. Sufficient Colorado River water shall be made available to Gila River users downstream
from Coolidge Dam. Compensation for losses of hydroelectric power at
Coolidge Power Plant shall be made from the Colorado River Development Fund.

3. In the event it is necessary to obtain modification of the decree of the
Supreme Court in *Arizona v. California*, the parties shall cooperate diligently to secure a modification accomplished by interstate compact or
by an amendment to the decree by the Court, whichever appears the
most appropriate procedure.

4. The Buttes Dam and Reservoir, a dam on the Gila to be built in conjunction with the CAP, shall be operated as not to prejudice the rights
of any users above the San Carlos Reservoir, as those rights are defined
under the Globe Equity Decree No. 59.

5. Arizona and New Mexico shall cooperate diligently in any way necessary to implement the principles set forth.[26]

The terms of the accord, along with a letter containing the concurrence
of Senator Anderson, were placed by Congressman Udall in the record of
the hearings held before the House subcommittee in May 1966 some time
subsequent to when Mr. Reynolds was a witness. Representing New Mexico, Mr. Reynolds registered the state's support of the CAP in anticipation
of successful completion of the Gila negotiations.[27] Very little was said about
the ongoing bargaining in the hearings. Congressman Aspinall simply
voiced his approval. He remarked:

> I am glad to recognize these acknowledged watermen from New Mex-
> ico, Mr. Reynolds and Mr. Coury. I am glad to hear about this friendly
> agreement between the states of New Mexico and Arizona. This is the
> way that the upper basin—or the lower basin as far as that is con-
> cerned—has had to settle their water controversies throughout the
> years, and this is just another example.[28]

The only other relevant remark made came appropriately from Congressman Udall. To Mr. Reynolds he said:

> We think you are a very able, very aggressive and a very statesmanlike
> representative of your people. We think you drive a hard bargain, but
> I want to confirm for the record what you said previously, that we are
> near agreement on these thorny and incredibly complex problems
> that have occupied so much time and attention along the Upper Gila.
> I express the hope you expressed, that in the immediate future, we
> would have some definite resolution of these so we could all go for-
> ward together.[29]

The final conclusion of the New Mexico–Arizona agreement was not,
however, achieved on quite the happy note struck at the hearings. Con-

gressman Udall proceeded to draft amendments to incorporate the settlement into the bill. The response of New Mexicans to the language suggested was stiffly negative. On May 26 a letter was addressed to Congressman Udall from Senator Anderson in which he reported:

> Steve Reynolds has pointed out to me that he had many reservations
> to the amendments as suggested by you. On this point he says, "Claude
> Mann, Harlan Flint, Dave Hale, Phil Mutz and I have carefully con-
> sidered these proposed amendments and have concluded that they
> do not accurately reflect the statement of principles of agreement con-
> tained in the May 12 memorandum to you from Congressmen Rhodes,
> Udall, and Senner."[30]

Mr. Reynolds's objections were directed to a number of provisions. He
felt that the amendment prohibiting the increase of the size of Hooker
Dam *prior* to importation had not been part of the original understanding.
Also, he did not comprehend the need to state in the amendments that
the water to be provided for exchanges was to come out of Arizona's entitlements. So, he sent Senator Anderson his own version of the amendments, and these were forwarded to Congressman Udall. In his document,
Mr. Reynolds provided that "construction of the Central Arizona Project
shall not be undertaken until and unless the states of Arizona and New
Mexico have ratified the Gila River System Compact." He then set out the
terms of the compact in a series of proposed amendments.[31]

On May 31, 1966, Congressmen Rhodes and Udall made a personal
appeal to Senator Anderson. They objected that Mr. Reynolds was trying
to escalate the conflict. The principles of May 11 had stated that either an
interstate compact or an amendment to the decree might be a method of
enforcing the agreement if a change in *Arizona v. California* were necessary,
yet now Mr. Reynolds was trying to specify a compact. They maintained
that such a veto power over the Central Arizona Project construction by
the New Mexico legislature which would have to ratify the compact would
create insurmountable problems for the Arizonans.[32]

In the phone calls and letters that followed, two agreements were quickly
arrived at. The Arizonans accepted the language of Mr. Reynolds governing increases of Hooker Dam. It was explained that the provision in Congressman Udall's proposed amendments stating that supplies for the exchanges required were to come from Arizona's entitlement was meant as
reassurance to other basin states that the Arizona–New Mexico accord
would not cost them any water. This clarification made the provision acceptable to Mr. Reynolds.

Reconciliation on the means to enforce the alteration of *Arizona v. California* division of Gila water was more difficult to achieve. After a great deal
of consideration, Arizona task force lawyers came to believe that Congress
had the power to authorize the secretary of the interior to contract with

New Mexico Gila users for water above the amount allotted to New Mexico by the Court. This made either a compact or an amendment to the decree unnecessary. To satisfy New Mexico representatives' desire for certainty on this point, Congressman Udall addressed a letter to his brother, the secretary, requesting an opinion from the department solicitor.[32] Mr. Ed Weinberg conferred informally with the Justice Department and determined that the authority of the legislation itself was sufficient to allow the secretary to contract with users in New Mexico for the state's new water.

As a postscript to the controversy, one small additional change was made in the agreement when the bill reached the Senate. Mr. Jerry Verkler, staff director of the Senate Committee on Interior and Insular Affairs, was a New Mexican who had been originally appointed to his post by Senator Anderson. He was one of Senator Anderson's advisors on water matters and took a particular interest in the construction of Hooker Dam. Thus, when the bill was taken up by the Senate in 1967, he became concerned upon examining the language agreed upon in 1966 that New Mexico was not fully protected. Under the specifications of a 98,000 acre-foot reservoir, Mr. Verkler feared that New Mexico would not be able to store sufficient supply to put her full 18,000 acre-feet of water to use. Rather than specify a size, he believed the language should simply state that Hooker Dam and Reservoir should be constructed in such a manner as to give effect to the agreement. Senator Anderson and Chief Engineer Reynolds were reluctant to reopen the dispute, but the Senate Committee staff director persisted.[34] Arizonans objected bitterly. From their point of view the state of New Mexico had the unpleasant habit of continually raising the price of its support for the CAP.[35] Nevertheless, the change was made.

Overview

The events recounted in this chapter make up a classic example of political bargaining. The Arizona–New Mexico negotiations were simply a matter of exchange—new water on the Gila for support or, at least, no obstruction of the Central Arizona Project. It was not a bargain which Arizona enjoyed making. In a joint press release, the Arizona congressmen characterized it as a "forced" agreement on principles.[36] Nevertheless, Arizona so desired the benefits of the bargain that she was willing to enter in. A shortage of time pressed heavily upon the Arizonans in the spring of 1966. The New Mexico support of the CAP completed the basinwide agreement. On top of the ordinary concern for getting through Congress the project Arizona so longed for, the Arizona activists wanted to take advantage of basin unity while the bargains struck to create it held together. And, as the history of legislation eventually proved, conservationist power was increasing as time wore on. Hearings in the House were not held until May, and once the bill passed the House, it still had to be taken up in the Senate. Accommodating Senator Anderson avoided one potential block in the way of the CAP in that body.

The majority-building problems faced by the Arizona activists represented power resources for the New Mexico negotiators. Timing was a strength in the New Mexico bargaining position. Without synchronizing their demands with the CAP, there would be no Hooker Dam or any new water for New Mexico. Senator Anderson's person and situation proved another example, similar to that of Congressman Aspinall in relation to the five Colorado projects, of the importance of a political activist to the success of a water proposal. The stake which Senator Anderson felt he had in the bill and his willingness to employ his resources or lend them to Mr. Reynolds were keys to bringing Arizona to the bargaining table.

This case puts the importance of law and politics in water matters into perspective. Law can create political controversy as well as settle it. The decree in *Arizona v. California* was intended to settle the division of Gila water. Although she was brought into the case against her will, it was New Mexico that requested the court to make an equitable apportionment. When New Mexico did not receive the amount of water wanted, the state appealed to the Congress, or to that part of the Congress involved in making water policy. And through the political process, New Mexico got the new water she wanted.

The behavior of representatives of states outside New Mexico and Arizona provide another insight into the political rules in the water game. Even though California Congressman Hosmer took Arizona's side in refusing to pay the price of New Mexico support, this support was simply verbal; Californians did not pressure New Mexico, for noninvolvement is the more typical stance of representatives not a part of the negotiations. When the agreement was reached, there were not even any inquiries from members of the House Interior Committee in the public record as to the terms of the agreement. Mutual noninterference was the political relationship among actors.

7

The Conservationist Challenge to New Mexico's Hooker Dam

Introduction

Hooker Dam was the vehicle designated by New Mexico whereby the 18,000 acre-feet won in the Arizona–New Mexico negotiations was to be put to use. The 215,000-acre-foot reservoir contemplated by State Engineer Reynolds promised southwestern New Mexico 10,800 acre-feet of new municipal and industrial water, 700 acre-feet of irrigation supply, and other benefits including, most importantly, recreation. The 6,400 acre-feet estimated to be lost by evaporation used up the rest of New Mexico's supplementary entitlement on the Gila. Thus, through Hooker Dam, the paper promise of new water on the Gila for New Mexico written into the Colorado River Basin Act was to be made secure by actually storing the supply and putting it to work in New Mexico.

The authorization of Hooker Dam in the Colorado River Basin Act as planned by New Mexico probably would have been accomplished smoothly and without controversy had it not contained one impediment. Construction at the Hooker site of a dam high enough to store the amount of water allocated in the bill to New Mexico would result in the backing of slack reservoir water across land within the Gila Primitive Area and through the Gila Gorge some seven to nine miles within the Gila Wilderness Area. The Gila Wilderness, the nation's oldest statutory wilderness, was established in 1924. It became a part of the wilderness system legislatively established by the Wilderness Act of 1964. Hooker Dam would be the first invasion of a wilderness by a reservoir since the passage of the Wilderness Act. Consequently, New Mexico's Hooker Dam stirred a conservationist hornets' nest. This chapter relates the manner in which New Mexico responded to the attack.

Conservationist Opposition

A peripheral invasion of a wilderness area in New Mexico was not the kind of issue to stir the broad national concern prompted by the central conservation issue of the Colorado River Basin Act—saving the Grand

Canyon. It was salient, instead, only to the zealous conservation organizations continually on guard against threats to areas set aside for preservation. The New Mexico Wildlife Federation, for instance, endorsed Hooker Dam, although it had opposed the Grand Canyon dams. In this battle, New Mexico was pitted not against a public outraged by an issue, but instead was confronted by the few really militant conservation groups that lacked the broad emotional response to Hooker Dam they got on the Grand Canyon dams.

Conservation organizations have a diversity of interests, and even the most zealous are not monolithic in their viewpoints nor unified in their responses to conservation issues. The two most involved conservation organizations in the Hooker fight, the Wilderness Society and the Sierra Club, saw different stakes in the issue and took stands sometimes at variance.

The positions of the Wilderness Society and the Sierra Club could be distinguished on several grounds and these differences traced to factors operating differentially on the two groups. There was a difference in the relative importance placed upon the Hooker battle vis-à-vis other conservation issues. A divergence existed as to whether Hooker Dam should be made a national campaign with a number of congressmen involved or kept as low-keyed pressure on the major activists. These major differences of priority and strategy resulted partly from the different kinds of support and information the two groups received in their efforts. To an extent, the groups depended on different activists, talked to different people, and learned different things.

The Wilderness Society saw in Hooker Dam an extreme hazard to its core interest, the wilderness preservation system. The greatest achievement for which the Wilderness Society could claim partial credit was the passage of the Wilderness Act in 1964. Its executive director for nineteen years, Howard Zahniser, was one of the principal architects of and tireless laborer for the wilderness bill. He died just four months before the president signed the act. Once the law was passed, the focus of the society shifted to protecting it in its most purely preservationist interpretation. The Wilderness Society has resisted various encroachments on the wilderness areas classified under the act. Further, it has tried to increase the amount of land so classified.

Hooker Dam struck a blow to the heart of the Wilderness Society's purpose. Consequently, it aroused an emotional reaction among the militants in the society. For them, the fate of the Gila was a bellwether. Stewart Brandborg, executive director of the Wilderness Society, told the House subcommittee in 1965:

> Now as a part of the national wilderness preservation system, the Gila is one of our most widely known national forest wilderness areas. Infringement of the Hooker Reservoir must be avoided if the national

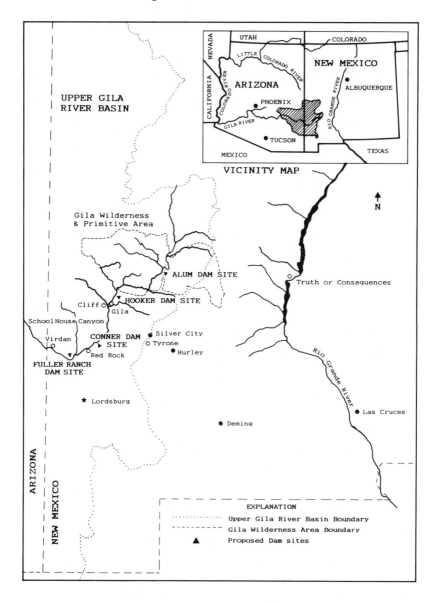

Proposed Construction on the Gila River

wilderness preservation system is not to be violated.[1]

The most basic concern of the Wilderness Society was the precedent-setting implications of Hooker Dam. At the same hearing, Mr. Brandborg stated that the Gila invasion along with the Grand Canyon dams would

"open the question of whether we in this Nation shall honor earlier dedi-
cations of lands that have been set aside for future generations of Amer-
icans."[2] More subtly, if Hooker Dam were allowed to encroach upon the
Gila Wilderness, it would be an unfortunate addition to the record of how
various ambiguous passages of the Wilderness Act were to be interpreted.
Under the legislation, certain of the multiple uses are allowed in wilderness if the president finds such use more in the national interest than pure
preservation. If Hooker Reservoir in the Gila Wilderness was found to be
in the national interest, why not a road or a mine somewhere else? Other
passages in the act, especially those relating to prospecting and mineral
extraction, were capable of a very loose interpretation. The Wilderness
Society was loath to begin to loosen the reins of very strict construction.

The strategy which the Wilderness Society settled upon was to offer an
alternative site for a dam on the Gila. In 1966, Stewart Brandborg suggested a list of different possibilities to the House subcommittee. By 1967,
Connor damsite had been selected as the most promising location. Mr.
Brandborg told the Senate subcommittee:

Located near Redrock, New Mexico, only 26 miles downstream from
the proposed Hooker Dam, the Connor project would intercept flood-
waters from several drainages downstream from Hooker. Because of
the substantially larger drainage area above it, the Connor Dam would
more than double the flood water catchment capacities of the proposed
Hooker project. . . . This reservoir would cover little farmland, but
would serve extensive downstream irrigation districts below Redrock,
New Mexico. Almost all of the lands covered by such a reservoir lie
within the Gila National Forest in an area where reservoir fishing,
boating, and fullest possible mass recreation uses and access could be
provided for nearby communities of New Mexico and Arizona. We
strongly urge that the Connor site be studied to fully determine its
flood control, reclamation, recreation and other benefits and that,
with the establishment of its feasibility, it be constructed as a practical
and acceptable means of preventing intrusion upon the Gila Wilderness Area and the national wilderness preservation system.[3]

This site was selected and supported for several reasons. One of the society's advisors with technical competence, who had visited the area of the
damsite, said it was a good one. Also it was the site which Mr. Claude Wood,
administrative assistant to Senator Anderson, preferred. To support a site
agreeable to a highly placed member of Senator Anderson's office seemed
good politics for the Wilderness Society.[4] Also the notion of an alternative
site appealed to Congressman John Saylor, who was a leading conservation
spokesman in the House and who had also been active in the Wilderness
Act campaign.[5]

The perspective of the Sierra Club was rather different from the Wilderness Society. Although both organizations vigorously opposed the Marble and Bridge dams, the Sierra Club had taken the leadership position in the Grand Canyon battle. It had invested tremendous amounts of time, energy, and money to force the huge hydroelectric units out of the Colorado River Basin Act. The Sierra Club had even had its tax-exempt status suspended by the Internal Revenue Service in 1966 because of its advertisements and other lobbying activities against the dams. The organization's stake in winning the fight was very great, and when the administration failed to recommend any dams in 1967 and the bill introduced in the 90th Congress by Senators Jackson and Hayden in the Senate contained none, the club felt victory nearly within its grasp. Sierra Club leaders were anxious to cooperate with the legislative process since it was working to the advantage of the Grand Canyon.

Distracted by the Grand Canyon, the Sierra Club determined to leave the Hooker matter to the Wilderness Society as far as Congress was concerned until May 1967. In his testimony at the Senate hearings in 1967, David Brower, executive director of the Sierra Club, treated the Hooker matter in a gingerly fashion:

> The efforts to dam the Grand Canyon and invade the national monument and park have a parallel in another part of the Colorado River basin legislation in which a dam is proposed, one suggested site of which would invade a unit of the wilderness preservation system.
>
> As a leader of the conservation movement—a leadership recognized by the Sierra Club when it made him an honorary life member—Senator Anderson well knows the depth of feeling held by all who fought with him for the wilderness system. We feel that if in these early years of operation of legislatively protected wilderness, there are breaches in protection of the system, then in later years these breaches will widen without check.
>
> One such threat is the plan of Kennecott Copper Corporation to gouge an open-pit mine out of the Glacier Peak Wilderness. This threat worries us as does the encroachment on the Gila Wilderness. We are worried because of the precedents, a very natural worry in this risky endeavor we call conservation.[6]

Mr. Jeffrey Ingram, Southwest representative of the Sierra Club and a major participant for the club in the Grand Canyon controversy, also skirted contention on Hooker Dam before the Senate subcommittee in 1967. He concluded his testimony:

> I would like to make one thing clear. This morning Senator Montoya made the statement that I was here to oppose Hooker Dam on behalf of the Save Grand Canyon Committee. At the time I responded, and I would just like to repeat that again, that I am here to make the state-

ment of the Save Grand Canyon Committee on the Grand Canyon only and not with any reference to Hooker Dam.[7]

The Save Grand Canyon Committee, an ad hoc group in New Mexico with a combined membership from many conservation organizations, was still fighting the Marble and Hualapai dams and had not come to a position on Hooker Dam. Shortly hereafter some of the members were to join the Gila Wilderness Study Group.

Unlike the Wilderness Society, the national Sierra Club was particularly aware of the opinions and interests of New Mexico. This sensitivity was reflected in relation to Senator Anderson. They believed that Senator Anderson was the key to any attempts to modify the plans for Hooker Dam. Consequently, it was important to maintain cordial relations and lines of communication. This concern was reflected in Mr. Brower's statement above, and was also displayed in an advertisement printed by the Gila Wilderness Study Group:

HELP SENATOR ANDERSON
SAVE THE GILA WILDERNESS
Senator Anderson helped establish the Gila Wilderness and was the leader in the fight for passage of the Wilderness Act. We must let him know that we support the preservation of the Wilderness Act. If we do not, then we cannot expect him to support the Gila against the Hooker Dam.[8]

Colonel Henry Zeller, U.S. Army retired, and Conservation Committee chairman of the Rio Grande chapter, was in frequent communication with Mr. Reynolds. He was aware of the state engineer's concern about Hooker Dam and opinion about the unacceptability of the Connor site. Mr. Zeller invested a great deal of time studying the Hooker proposal and came to the conclusion that any dam was uneconomic and unnecessary. It was his position that the opposition of the Sierra Club should be to any large dam on the Gila.[9]

The position of the Sierra Club was also affected by the taste of its involved members concerning the quality of the land to be inundated. None of the Sierra Club members agreed with the proponents of Hooker damsite that the area to be covered was "a tiny segment of the wilderness now subjected to flooding and erosion, leaving only sandbars and gravel piles enjoyed by no one, not even wildlife."[10] One enthusiast of the place described it as follows:

The area in question, whether four or ten miles is of definite scenic interest. The rock is colored, at times brilliantly. The sculpturing of the walls varies from the angular blockiness to intricate smoothness. The number of trees make part of the river bottom a virtual forest.[11]

Mile 23.5 of the Gila Gorge country that the proposed Hooker Dam would inundate. Photo by John McComb.

At the same time, many New Mexicans who had hiked along the Gila River, including the author of the above description, could not say that the area which waters would engulf under a reservoir at the Connor site was less beautiful. For this reason, many conservation activists in New Mexico were loath to choose which piece of land to sacrifice and preferred not recommending any particular site. The Southwest representative of the Sierra Club wrote to a conservationist volunteer:

> I don't believe we can in good conscience oppose Hooker by backing an alternate site. That means that we either find another way of accomplishing the goals Hooker would—and I don't know how this would be done—or we simply oppose the invasion of the first Wilderness ever set aside.[12]

Defenders of Hooker in New Mexico

A pocket of adamant defenders of Hooker Dam existed in southwestern New Mexico, particularly in Silver City and adjacent communities. These local interests supplied energetic grassroots support for the construction.

The Southwestern Damsiters or the Hooker Dam Association had been founded in 1957 for the explicit purpose of urging water resource development. Members of the group believed themselves to have been hard hit by the Supreme Court decision dividing Gila water and dedicated themselves to achieving more extensive water use by a dam on the mainstream.[13] Mr. Alvin Franks of Silver City was the prime mover and president of this organization. Mr. Franks successfully generated support from civic organizations and community government throughout Grants and Luna counties. Among the numerous letters for New Mexicans in support of Hooker Dam inserted into the record of the 1967 Senate hearings, many are addressed to Mr. Franks or the Damsiters or referred to them.[14]

Insofar as the most prominent local supporters anticipated a single, concrete benefit to be achieved by Hooker Reservoir, it was recreation.[15] A state legislator from the area expressed his hopes in a letter to Senator Anderson:

> We are close enough to several large cities that such a recreation outlet would mean many dollars to us and the state of New Mexico. As it is now, the people from El Paso and Las Cruces go right on through to lakes galore in Arizona.
>
> This section of New Mexico feels that we certainly need a large body of water that can be made into a real recreation area. There are such areas in the central and northern parts of the state but we do not have such a luxury down here.[16]

Recreation benefits could be achieved wherever the dam was located, and some of the local backers did not care where the dam was placed.[17] If the reservoir were located at the Hooker site, however, a road through Silver City would be the only easy access to the reservoir. Consequently, the members of the Hooker Dam Association, concentrated in Silver City, had a particular attachment to the site.

Changing the site to accommodate the wilderness concept rankled many southwestern New Mexicans who had little attachment to it. Mr. Alvin Franks expressed his own view:

> Our wilderness laws, as they now stand, must either be changed or some day our wilderness areas will be lost. The benefits of Hooker are pretty well established. The advantages and disadvantages of our Wilderness Act are not understood. A meeting to discuss the pros and cons of the wilderness law, the problems of administering it, the cost to the taxpayer, the loss of the revenue from these all-important areas, the ill effects upon the forest and how it retards the use for people might be in order.[18]

Cattlemen in the Gila area had objected strongly to the establishment of the Gila Primitive Area.[19] Classification of the primitive area into the wilderness was to come up for review in 1971 within the Forest Service. The Silver City *Daily Press* suggested that if the people of Silver City should lose the Hooker project because of conservation opposition they might well oppose the inclusion of the primitive area into the wilderness.[20]

The local support reinforced the public officials active in defending Hooker Dam, most notably, State Engineer Reynolds and Senator Anderson. Mr. Reynolds had invested considerable time and energy in extracting from Arizona the additional 18,000 acre-feet above the entitlement given by the Supreme Court. Hooker Dam was intended to make the victory really secure by putting that water to use. For Mr. Reynolds, achieving additional water in the Colorado River Basin Act was a now or never proposition. He wrote to the southwest representative of the Sierra Club:

> As I have said to you before, the prospect that we can put to use the additional water we would be given a right to by the pending legislation is not nebulous, but is rather a virtual certainty. It is also certain that, if the legislation authorizing the Central Arizona Project does not give us a right to additional water from the Gila River system, we will never get that right and will be forever limited to our present uses from the system.[21]

The conservationist opposition to Hooker, arising as it did late in the legislative process, threatened to disturb all the achievements of the Arizona–New Mexico settlement of the Gila. It was not in Mr. Reynolds's interest to entertain interruptions to the smooth authorization of the project. To open up the question of the exact location of the dam invited controversy in southwestern New Mexico and questions in Congress and the administration about the characteristics of the project. The project plan was very old and had only been superficially updated. Only the Hooker site on the Gila had been really investigated. The state engineer did not have the data available to choose and justify an alternative to the Hooker site.

The exact location of a storage dam on the Gila was not as important as the total amount of water which would accrue to New Mexico. Mr. Reynolds was convinced that evaporation at the Connor site, where the reservoir would spread over a larger area, would be substantially greater than at the Hooker site. Also, because the drainage area to the Connor damsite was larger, the dam was expected to silt up more rapidly. The result would be a greater cost per acre-foot of water stored, an expense which Mr. Reynolds was reluctant to incur. He claimed the Connor Reservoir would inundate some 900 acres of farmland as well.

Mr. Reynolds's contacts and communications with the opposition occurred with conservationists in his own state associated with the Sierra Club. He had lengthy correspondence and a few public confrontations with Mr. Zeller and Mr. Ingram. He was aware that these men doubted the advisability of any dam on the Gila at any location. He was convinced of the correctness of his position in pursuing new water for New Mexico and supplied data and answered questions readily on the supposition that information ultimately would support his position.[22]

Senator Clinton P. Anderson was the most important champion of Hooker Dam. Without doubt it was his influence which achieved for New Mexico new water on the Gila. It is equally certain that his commitment to the Hooker project at the proposed site saved the dam in the legislative process. The reasons for Mr. Anderson's commitment to Hooker are complex and difficult to unravel. The real explanation probably can be found only in the man and his individual thought processes. The research can only suggest some factors which contributed to his stand.

Senator Anderson's sponsorship of the Wilderness Act and his dedication to shepherding it through Congress established his reputation as a conservationist. Secretary Udall testified to this and to the privilege he felt this afforded the senator at the Senate subcommittee hearings in 1967:

> Senator, may I add one other thing for the record here, because those who know the history of the wilderness bill, and your leadership in it, ought to know, too, that your own personal ties with the wilderness with this particular piece of wilderness, that this is where your convictions arise from. I think again, I would be very disappointed in the preservation people, in the conservation movement, if they don't look with a little bit of flexibility on your own views with regard to a problem of this kind, because no one has a deeper commitment nor has done more for the Wilderness Society than you.[23]

Senator Anderson was obviously piqued by the questioning of his wilderness sense in regard to Hooker Dam. He felt stung by what he regarded as ungrateful letters from conservationists. These feelings served to separate Senator Anderson from the conservationists and caused him to discount their opinions. To a student who had written in protest of Hooker Dam, Senator Anderson answered:

> I have discussed your letter with a friend of mine who knows the situation, and his comment was that "when that young man has done as much for conservation as you have, he might have a right to talk."
>
> I am not that severe, but I do think that you might have checked to see just what this problem involves. When the Gila monument was dedicated, the conservation groups asked me to make an address; and I flew down there with them and enjoyed the occasion very much because I am very enthusiastic about the Gila Wilderness. At the time when there were strong sentiments to change the boundaries of the Gila Wilderness I was the only public official, so far as I know, who stood up and fought the cattlemen hour after hour.[24]

Senator Anderson felt that the conservationists were so purist and inflexible, as evidenced by the Hooker case, that they threatened to make the Wilderness Act unworkable. He advised his conservationist correspondents that a balanced approach must be taken in the conservation of resources. All of the facets in each particular instance must be examined and judged against a standard of what is the highest public value to be attained. This, he said, was what he was trying to do in weighing all the aspects of the Hooker controversy.[25] "If all these contentions [of the conservationists] prove that the areas in wilderness are so tightly confined that no gallon of water from a dam can reach any part of the wilderness system, we have serious trouble on that score."[26]

Looking at the facts and balancing them in relation to Hooker Dam, Senator Anderson came to the conclusion that what was to be sacrificed was not of great significance. In the Senate hearings, he referred to the damsite as just an ordinary gravel bank.[27] The senator frequently used gravel in describing the Hooker site. In one case he said:

There are a great many acres in the Gila Wilderness and the Gila Primitive Area that might not measure up to the concept you have of wilderness. The Hooker Dam site is just one of them. It has no particular scenic beauty. It is, instead, an ordinary river bed which largely features miles of gravel and scrub vegetation.[28]

The senator disputed scenic photos sent to him as not really having been taken in the Hooker Reservoir area.

Senator Anderson threatened several times in the course of the controversy that if the conservationists continued their objections, the statutory protections would simply be removed from the reservoir area. To Mr. Zeller, the conservation chairman of the Sierra Club, the senator wrote:

I intend, if the present objections continue, to see if I can prevail on the proper officials to carve out from the Gila Primitive Area or the Wilderness Area the 134 acres that seem to be causing all the trouble.

I, at least, have visited the area, and I think if others visited it, each might find that the area in question is pretty much of a large size gravel pit along the banks of the river. I never dreamed that after all the hard work I did in regard to the Wilderness Bill that I would be confronted with the necessity of altering the boundaries of the Gila Primitive Area to let a badly needed dam be constructed. I cannot believe that objections to the Hooker Dam are the last word; but if the conservationists insist, I have no alternative.[29]

Against the not very great sacrifice of wilderness he perceived, Senator Anderson balanced the very considerable advantages of Hooker Dam as he saw them. He had long been dedicated to a dam on the Gila. In one of his early congressional campaigns, he had promised southwestern New

Mexicans that he would work hard to get a dam at the Hooker site.[30] In his capacity as subcommittee chairman, Senator Anderson began the Senate hearings in 1967 by saying he could not overemphasize his support for the Hooker proposal. He maintained that the project was located in an area of New Mexico which needed full and wise development of water resources to trigger the maximum use of minerals and other resources.[31]

Where the project was to be specifically located seemed not to concern Senator Anderson as long as the place chosen was the best site. He ultimately became convinced that Connor was an unacceptable site.[32] Evaporation at the downstream location was prohibitively high, and pumping costs of water to Silver City would be higher.

History of the Controversy

Something like a focus on the conservation issues posed by Hooker Dam did not occur in Congress until the House hearings of 1968, very late in the tortuous history of the Colorado River Basin Act. The Wilderness Society mentioned the issue in 1965 and 1966. In 1966, Mr. Brandborg's testimony suggesting a number of alternate sites was inserted at the end of the *Hearings*. State Engineer Reynolds rebutted the virtues contended for alternate sites in a letter sent to House subcommittee chairman Johnson April 6, 1967. He concluded in this letter that Bureau of Reclamation studies in 1930 and 1963 had shown the Hooker site to be better than any downstream alternatives, including Connor. He claimed that recreation and fishing benefits at the Hooker reservoir would more than offset the small infringement on the Gila Wilderness.[33] Except for the usual Wilderness Society testimony against Hooker Dam, little happened in the House in 1967. The Senate subcommittee hearings in 1967 were conducted under the watchful eyes of subcommittee chairman Anderson. Both the Wilderness Society and the Sierra Club testified against the precedent of wilderness invasion, but the statements were largely passed over. In the hearings record, whatever the conservationists said was more than offset by the remarks of Senator Joseph Montoya, Democrat of New Mexico, Alvin Franks, S. E. Reynolds, and above all, the secretary of the interior, Stewart Udall, all totally agreeing with Senator Anderson. At one point the secretary said:

> Senator, I want to go on record on this point. I think this can very accurately be described as a very peripheral wilderness involvement. I think we must be flexible enough concerning the wilderness system, because we are going to see, from time to time, problems like this arise, to be able to modify boundaries, and to exclude small areas, particularly where a minimum peripheral invasion is involved. We should be flexible, and perhaps compensate by putting a little more land in the wilderness area elsewhere. . . . I think this is sound from a con-

servation point of view. I must say I disagree with those who oppose Hooker Dam because I think it is a de minimis thing with those of my friends in the wilderness movement who want to make every acre that once goes into it sacred.[34]

Practically nothing was said in the Senate hearings by any committee member except Senator Anderson about the Hooker Dam controversy. At one point during Mr. Reynolds's appearance, Senator Allott remarked:

Then the committee here does have to make a determination and policy whether or not we will adhere strictly to the provisions of the wilderness bill, which the distinguished chairman of this committee, this subcommittee, was such an ardent advocate of, or whether we can permit just a little invasion and a little modification of the wilderness areas.[35]

After stating the dilemma, the Colorado senator did not go on to take a position or even pursue the issue.

In settings other than the hearings, senators proved no more willing to involve themselves in what was conceived of as Senator Anderson's concern.[36] The Hooker provision escaped the committee markup unscathed. Both Wilderness Society and Sierra Club representatives visited senators and the Sierra Club staff mostly in behalf of the Grand Canyon. The southwestern representative of the club said he mentioned Hooker in visits to senators and their staff, but received little positive response. Senators Phillip A. Hart, Democrat from Michigan, and William Proxmire, Democrat from Wisconsin, did mention the wilderness invasion in speeches on the Senate floor, but no debate or amendments affecting Hooker ensued.[37]

Between the Senate hearings and the 1968 House hearings, conservationists mounted their campaign. The Wilderness Society generated mail. A Wilderness Society report sent to members stated that Hooker was a first test of the Wilderness Act. The Colorado Open Space Coordinating Council sent out a flyer urging the Connor site. Senator Anderson's office stated that before this publicity the senator had received a total of fifty to sixty letters, and since, the Hooker mail had averaged six to eight communications a day.[38]

New Mexico conservationists centered their energies on Senator Anderson. Besides the Gila Study Group's advertisement urging polite letters to the senior senator, conservation leaders themselves wrote him. New Mexico conservationists urged the senator to visit the site of the dam with them. For a time, he was receptive to the notion, but Congress remained in session through the summer and he was unable to make the trip.

New Mexico conservationists finally achieved a personal interview with Senator Anderson on December 28, 1967. After an hour and three-quarters of discussion, neither the senator nor the critics of Hooker Dam were much

moved. A series of amendments was suggested by the conservationists:
1. Providing the dam be located so as not to infringe on the wilderness.
2. Providing no money be appropriated until after the National Water Commission submits its recommendation.
3. Providing the president first finds the wilderness invasion in the national interest.
4. Providing no appropriations until a feasibility study is completed and the provisions of the Wilderness Act relating to the finding of national interest have been complied with.[39]

The senator rejected the lot.

The Issue Compromised

As the action which Chairman Aspinall promised would occur early in the second session of the 90th Congress approached, it became obvious that something would have to be done about conservation opposition to Hooker if the bill were to proceed smoothly. Congressman John Saylor, the ranking minority member on the House committee, was preparing to make a fight on the issue. In October, he transmitted a list of forty-two questions which he had received from the New Mexico conservationists to the Bureau of Reclamation for consideration. Senator Anderson's office and State Engineer Reynolds requested the bureau to check all answers with them that were sent to Mr. Saylor.[40] All the questions and answers were inserted into the record of the abbreviated hearings held in the House from January 1 through February 2 of 1968, when only departmental officials appeared.[41] This incipient threat to upset the combination in support of the CAP could not long be ignored by those committed to its passage.

Congressman Morris Udall viewed the Hooker matter with mixed feelings. He had accepted the project to satisfy Senator Anderson and had no other connection to it. The Arizona Hiking Club, with a membership in his district, had ventured into the Gila Wilderness and extolled its beauty. On the other hand, Senator Anderson had the reputation of understanding wilderness. Morris Udall hesitated to question the New Mexico senator's judgment, especially when Senator Anderson's help on the CAP was so badly needed.[42] Further, the conservationists' inflexibility on this matter disturbed Congressman Udall. He told them that when 99 percent of the conservation battle in the basin bill had been won, as it had been with the defeat of the Grand Canyon dams, it was foolish to "chuck" your friends for the last 1 percent.[43]

Some sort of action was called for, Mr. Udall believed, if a damaging confrontation was to be avoided on Hooker. Consequently, he took up the task of facilitating a compromise between Senator Anderson and the conservationists. In conversations with Jerry Verkler, a close advisor to Anderson, he found that little possibility existed for accommodation of opposing positions. Connor site was definitely unacceptable. Taking the reservoir land out of the primitive and wilderness classification and substituting other land was acceptable to Anderson but completely unacceptable to the Wilderness Society. The New Mexico conservationists were willing to permit the president to make the final decision by requiring a presidential finding that the dam was in the national interest, taking the wilderness values into consideration. Senator Anderson took the view, however, that the president had already approved the project in the act by recommending the project to Congress along with the CAP.[44]

After a complex process of checking and double-checking with Senator Anderson, Mr. Reynolds, and conservationists in New Mexico, Congressman Udall settled upon compromise language. Hooker Dam, *or suitable alternative,* was to be authorized in the CAP. Senator Anderson had always maintained that he wanted the Bureau of Reclamation to study the matter thoroughly and build the best project. Since studies had not yet really been accomplished, the language was reasonable to the senior senator.[45] State Engineer Reynolds concurred. He had felt all along that lack of study or information on Hooker was the weakest part of New Mexico's case.

Neither the Wilderness Society nor the principal congressional spokesman for the conservationists, Congressman John P. Saylor, found the language of the Udall compromise sufficiently strong. The substitution of "Connor or suitable alternative" was much to be preferred, and Congressman Saylor determined to support an amendment in the subcommittee and full committee markup sessions. Congressman Saylor could muster only eight votes for the Connor amendment in the Reclamation subcommittee. Congressman Udall was one of the fifteen votes against the amendment. He maintained he had pushed Senator Anderson as far as he would go on the matter of compromising Hooker. Connor would never be accepted by the senator in conference. Further, the New Mexico conservationists found the language "Hooker or suitable alternative" acceptable.[46] Following this defeat of the Connor amendment, the Udall compromise, supported by Congressman Saylor, was accepted by the subcommittee. Similar events occurred in the full committee markup when the Connor amendment likewise was defeated eleven to ten.

A decision made by Congressman Saylor to press for the Connor amendment on the House floor was bolstered by the fact that seventeen members, a bare majority of the House Interior Committee, signed a strongly worded minority report against the Hooker site.[47] How Congressman Saylor could collect a majority for his report while he had been defeated at the committee is something of a puzzle. One explanation might have been the strong efforts made by representatives of the Wilderness Society and other conservation groups in Washington to collect signatures for the report.[48] Another possible explanation was the willingness of the northwesterners on the committee to go along with Representative Saylor even though they cared little about the issue. Since an importation study provision was in the House bill, the outnumbered representatives from the Pacific Northwest states were willing "to throw sand in the gears" grinding out the bill at every opportunity.[49] Congressman Saylor did not really expect to win a vote on the House floor for the Connor site, but he decided to try anyway, because "there was always the chance."[50] He did not think the "Connor or suitable alternative" amendment would be accepted by Senator Anderson in conference if it did pass the House.

The decision of Congressman Saylor to continue the conflict presented difficult problems for Congressman Udall. The Arizonan wanted to avoid confrontation. He tried to convince conservationists to drop the matter. In order to convince them, he supplied his own loose interpretation of "or suitable alternative" and attempted unsuccessfully to have a broad interpretation written into the House committee report for the majority.[51] Attempts to persuade New Mexicans to accept Connor or to compromise further proved fruitless. Mr. Reynolds believed if "Connor or suitable alternative" became law, Hooker, because it invaded the wilderness, would never be seriously considered. To recommend Hooker in this circumstance would require a new presidential finding of national interest in encroachment on the wilderness.[52] Congressman Udall was terribly worried that the Hooker matter would divide the support for the CAP and jeopardize passage of the bill.[53]

New Mexico conservationists, particularly the Southwest representative of the Sierra Club, felt torn in this situation. There was a desire to support Congressman Saylor and remain united with the Wilderness Society. At the same time, a kind of obligation existed to support Congressman Udall and the compromise he had managed to achieve. In addition, there was no particular attachment on the part of New Mexico conservationists for the Connor site. It would never be accepted by Mr. Reynolds and Senator Anderson; it was less feasible and still sacrificed scenic values. New Mexico conservationists hoped that finally an alternative to any large dam on the Gila could be found.

Ultimately the leadership of the Sierra Club, prompted by the Southwest representative, attempted to dissuade Congressman Saylor from offering his amendment. David Brower, the executive director, sent a telegram as follows:

> As floor debate approaches on Central Arizona Project, we are seriously questioning advisability of an amendment to substitute Connor for Hooker Dam. New Mexico conservationists feel present language, if broadly interpreted, will suffice to kill Hooker. Because of "or suitable alternative" language, we feel legal basis for fighting Hooker administratively is not improved by change to Connor. We believe a way has been found to assure a broad-based study by the Secretary without introducing the name Connor Dam, and therefore we feel that

further amendment is not necessary.

I have asked Jeff Ingram, our specialist on the Hooker problem, to try to reach you by phone on Friday to discuss this matter.[54]

In spite of the break in the ranks of his supporters, Congressman Saylor pursued his course. During the May 14, 1968, House debate on the CAP, the Pennsylvania Republican offered his amendment, "Connor or suitable alternative." Congressman Udall rose in opposition to the amendment. He pointed out that under the Saylor language Hooker might well be chosen a suitable alternative. He also noted that the Sierra Club did not insist upon the amendment. The gist of his argument is indicated in the following excerpt from the debate:

> If the members of the committee please, I suggest again we are not really arguing over any matter of great substance. In either event there will be a study. There will be a final look at this. There will be an op- portunity, when appropriations are sought, to review this matter again, regardless of the decision which is made.
>
> So I would prefer and I would suggest that in this situation we stay with the committee and we stay with the people of New Mexico.
>
> I want to commend their leaders in this House and in the other body for the attitude they have taken on this matter. There has been a lot of national publicity about this. But New Mexico has said, "We do not want to invade the wilderness. We hope there is an alternative. We hope that another way can be found to do this job."
>
> In this situation, where there is no real distinction between the ef- fect of the amendment of the language of the bill, I hope this commit- tee will stay with New Mexico. We do not have to have this argument now. We can settle it later down the line.[55]

The members of the House were evidently in accord with Congressman Udall's view. On a teller vote, the Connor amendment was turned down forty-five to eighty-nine.[56]

As Senator Anderson had agreed, the language on Hooker recommended by the House-Senate conference committee and accepted in both bodies was the House language, "Hooker or suitable alternative." Without the support of a vote in his favor in the House, Congressman Saylor had little with which to oppose Senator Anderson. The issue was swallowed up by the larger issues of geopolitics in the conference committee.[57]

Overview

New Mexico won the controversy over Hooker Dam. New Mexico sup- porters of water development certainly achieved a victory. The project with the addition of a few qualifying words stayed in the bill despite the threat of the conservationists. In a lesser sense, New Mexico conservationists also experienced a gain. They assured themselves an opportunity to fight further, in the framework of the administration, against a wilderness invasion or any large dam on the Gila. They hoped that through their prodding of the Bureau of Reclamation and the secretary of the interior some other preferable altenative would be chosen.

The fundamental cause of both victories was Senator Anderson. His powers afforded him the right to choose, and the compromise "or suitable alternative" was one with which he was comfortable. Of course, Congressman Udall played an important role here as a kind of conduit of compromise. Some sort of communications link was necessary between the House, the conservationists, and the senator. Udall performed the job in the service of the CAP, rather than from any concern about the issue.

If it had not been that his own vital goals were at stake, Congressman Udall would probably have followed the pattern of noninterference set by other legislators in regard to the Hooker matter. Senators on and off the committee with only a few exceptions remained aloof from the controversy. This was considered Senator Anderson's affair. More remote from Senator Anderson's sphere of influence, House members ventured some involvement in the issue in greater numbers than in the Senate. A majority did sign the dissenting views on Hooker in the committee report. A few members of Congress spoke against Hooker on the floor. However, the enthusiasm for the conservation issue visible in the Grand Canyon dams battle was lacking as evidenced by the final tally vote on the Saylor amendment. The prevailing viewpoint was generally expressed in a remark made by Chairman Aspinall on the floor to the effect that the whole matter would ultimately be settled in conference where Senator Anderson would have a large say.[58]

The major exception to mutual noninterference as the most common stance on Hooker was, of course, Congressman John P. Saylor. He was, by his own admission, something of a maverick in water politics.[59] He had little constituency interest in water development policy and consequently had a great deal of leeway. One of the roles in Congress he chose to espouse was that of conservation spokesman. He played this part often—in the Echo Park controversy in 1956, in the passage of the Wilderness bill in 1964, and in the Grand Canyon dams fight. His freedom in choosing the role carried with it a burden of the lack of local support. His information and backing came from national conservation groups, not local interests. Ordinarily, as in the Hooker case, water development decisions were detemined on a local level. The distance which separated Congressman Saylor and the New Mexico conservationists illustrated this point. New Mexico conservationists focused upon the leverage points which they believed would determine the issue—local residents, state water officials, and Senator Anderson. In doing so, they came to cross-purposes with Congressman Saylor who responded simply to the principle of the Wilderness Act and depended upon a national reaction. This national interest in the Hooker issue, of course, did not materialize.

The case of the Hooker controversy points up some of the difficulties conservation groups had in affecting water development policy. Where a national publicity campaign could not be successfully mounted, as in this issue, conservationists had few resources for influence. To be successful here, the local people would have had to have been convinced of the value of wilderness. Conservationists would have had to have a powerful, locally based political activist committed to their cause. Strong conservation sentiments in New Mexico would have had to change the political environment of State Engineer Reynolds and Senator Anderson, forcing them to consider alternatives to invasion of the wilderness. The actual state of affairs was that southwestern New Mexicans badly wanted the project while other residents, with the exception of the conservationists, were not aroused.

The Hooker controversy also indicated the difficulty conservation groups had in negotiations. They found themselves in bargaining situations being asked to compromise their core interests. The Wilderness Society could not in good conscience see a part of the Gila Wilderness carved out for Hooker, even if it were replaced by some other area. Likewise, the New Mexico conservationists were loath to sacrifice the scenic beauty of the Connor site in exchange for no dam at the Hooker location.

The result of the conservationists' national, rather than local, constituency, their reliance on the tools of mass publicity campaigns, and their reluctance to bargain with the land, was that the entrance of conservationists into water politics ordinarily signaled disruption. The delicate negotiations necessary to build majorities for water projects were unsettled. Conflict damaging to the successful completion of the legislative process on a project or package of projects erupted. This meant tremendous trouble to the activist committed to getting a project through Congress. Understandably, congressmen who labored to acquire water development for their areas often viewed the contribution of conservationists bitterly.

8

Lessons Drawn in 1968

Introduction

The passage of time frequently contributes the distance necessary to appropriately assess the relative importance of past events. It is commonly argued that assessments made immediately after a significant occurrence are too early to identify the lasting lessons. On the other hand, the passage of time dulls the sharpness of impressions and increases the temptation of the analyst to reinterpret the past in order to better justify current positions and preferences. The first chapter of this book reflects the longer overview of the constants in the pattern of water resources that have persisted from the case study period in the 1960s through the 1980s. Whatever perspective and wisdom come with the passage of two decades is reflected in the first chapter. This eighth chapter was written immediately after the Colorado River Basin Act was passed. Any tendency to modify past insights to better support what are identified as enduring lessons in the first chapter has been effectively checked by this reproduction of conclusions as they were seen at the time.

The Pervasiveness of Politics

The role of New Mexico in relation to the Colorado River Basin Act illustrates the overriding significance of political feasibility in determining water policy. New Mexico's water development plans were included in the basin legislation on the basis of political calculation. For the activists committed to the authorization of the Central Arizona Project, the cost of refusing projects in New Mexico was too great to incur. Justifications other than politics had little influence in determining this policy. Where the politically rational action of accommodating New Mexico could be bolstered by economic and other supports, the arguments were made. Where the results of these criteria did not help to justify what was politically feasible, they were ignored, overriden, or tampered with so that the conclusions they turned up were politically viable.

In the case of the Animas–La Plata Project, the economic test was subsidiary to political imperatives. The compelling justification for including the project in the basin bill was Chairman Wayne Aspinall's commitment to it. This dedication derived from his own perception of the risks and opportunities confronted by Colorado in the basin bill. To protect Colorado's water, he wanted to see all of it put to use at the same time the Central Arizona Project went into operation. Whether this project and the other four Colorado projects were the best way to employ his state's water resources or were even economically justifiable as a national undertaking was not politically relevant. The point was that these projects, for various reasons, were next in line for authorization in Colorado. To comply with the formal requirements of benefit/cost analysis, the benefits supposedly to be derived from the Animas–La Plata Project were reallocated to some degree, but it is important to note that this change was made because of the political necessity of justifying the project, not because of immediate demands for additional municipal and industrial supplies.

The capacity of a project to survive an orderly process of clearance and review which brings a number of relevant interests into decision making is supposed to insure the all-around soundness of a project. The clearance and review of the revised Animas–La Plata Project testified mainly to the strength of the political support behind it. Clearly, for example, California's change of mind on the project had little to do with its characteristics or their revision. Rather, the turnabout attested to a changed political situation in which it was important for California that Congressman Aspinall be accommodated. Besides the pro forma review which agencies and states gave the project because of the strong pressure for positive action, the ordinary time schedule was radically readjusted at every point along the clearance route. Thus, the authorization process as a way of justification, in the case of Animas–La Plata, was twisted out of joint by the overriding political justification for the project.

It was a legal settlement which was set aside on account of politics in the Arizona–New Mexico negotiations on the Gila. Whatever language in the settlement in *Arizona v. California* to which New Mexico could refer to justify reopening the question of the division of water on the Gila, Arizona was in the stronger legal position in that she could refer to the substance of the decree itself. In substance, the special master had given New Mexico only around 31,000 acre-feet of water per year, an amount agreed to by stipulation of both parties. New Mexico was much stronger in the political framework of the Colorado River Basin Act than she had been in the legal framework of the Supreme Court case. Consequently, she reopened the issue in this other arena and achieved a settlement much more to her liking than she had gotten in court.

An act of Congress establishing wilderness areas for the purpose of preservation was bent to accommodate the political feasibility of Hooker Dam. The central purpose of the Wilderness Act of 1964 has been to preserve the land in its natural state untouched by humans. By no leap of the imagination is a slack water reservoir, where once there was a running stream, nature at its most natural. Of course, there are a number of elastic clauses in the Wilderness Act which can be stretched to allow some other uses for wilderness besides maintaining the land unimpaired. It takes political prowess to do the stretching, however, since the spirit of the act is contrary to such encroachment. New Mexico had this political strength in regard to Hooker Dam.

Since political feasibility is as important to policy making in water as any economic or engineering criteria, it follows that political scientists can contribute as substantially as do other disciplines to the understanding of water development. While economists and engineers have thoroughly established and refined their tests of water policy, political scientists have only begun to explore the pattern of politics in this issue area. The purpose of this study has been to build a political model of water policy and then to measure its relevance and explanatory power in the case of New Mexico's role in the Colorado River Basin Act.

Adequacy of the Model

The pattern of politics set forth in chapter 3 provides a framework which fits quite well the cases examined here. The most significant influences in legislating the Colorado River Basin Act, including the provisions affecting New Mexico, were also identified as the main factors in the model. According to the pattern, the most important attribute of water policy is its basis in the locality. The motivating drive for a water project comes from the area where it is believed that the benefits will accrue. In the cases of the Animas–La Plata Project and Hooker Dam, a strong thrust emanated from the localities toward the authorization of the projects. The La Plata Conservancy Districts in New Mexico and Colorado and the Hooker Dam Association all had long-standing attachments toward the water development they believed would be a real boon to the localities.

According to the model, strong local sentiments create certain risks and rewards for locally based political actors. These locally oriented activists find it in their best interest to become involved in the issue, and they are the prime movers in shaping water development policy. The core activists on Animas–La Plata, on the division of Gila water, and on the authorization of Hooker Dam, were all political actors whose support came from localities and who had perceived an important stake in effecting water development policy. State Engineer Reynolds, Senator Anderson, and Congressman Aspinall must be credited with the degree of success New Mexico achieved in the Colorado River Basin Act. The attachment they had for specific projects and the sort of political influence they wielded provided the political feasibility which accounted for the inclusion of the projects.

The pattern set out in chapter 3 suggests that Congress is most likely to be the locus of activity on water policy. The locally oriented activists in water will, according to the model, focus their energies upon institutions in the political system where sufficient authority resides to make policy and where locally based activists have the best access and the largest share of power resources. Congress was found to be the focus of activity on the projects in New Mexico. The Animas–La Plata Project was wrenched from the administrative framework in which it was pursuing the long route to positive recommendation and injected into the congressional process on the Colorado River Basin Act. This occurred when Congressman Aspinall, whose political resources were in Congress, determined it was to his advantage to get immediate action on the project. The decision as to the division of Gila water was taken out of the legal framework of the Court, where it was thought by Arizonans the issue had been settled, and remade by bargaining in a congressional setting. The power to move the issue from one arena to another derived from the political resources which Senator Anderson had in Congress, particularly in relation to the Colorado River Basin Act.

In the authorization of Hooker Dam which threatened to back up reservoir water into the Gila Wilderness, Congress was the focus of activity in altering wilderness policy which it had previously made in the Wilderness Act of 1964. The policy-making process in Congress on water development is continuous, where shifts in the distribution of power among activists are repeatedly registered in a new policy.

The pattern of politics on water development traced in chapter 3 identifies mutual noninterference as a consent-building relation. The live-and-let-live attitude of such a relation fits the lack of shared interest which various locally based activists experience vis-à-vis one another. It is also compatible with the formal and informal rules of Congress. Noninterference fits nicely with what was observed in the case studies. The most relevant question for the supporters of the CAP was whether the inclusion of New Mexico's demands added necessary support to the package of which the CAP was the core. Where such political feasibility existed, no further questions were asked. The operative assumptions among congressmen involved in the basin bill seems to have been that the way a state puts its entitlement to use is its own affair, provided everyone agrees the water can be used by that state without jeopardizing others. Implicit here is the further assumption that noninterference will be paid back in kind. Water development projects, consequently, are treated as quite discrete problems concerning mainly the locality and local representatives, the proof of which is the strength of support they generate.

In the model, conflict in the pattern of politics on water is avoided by accommodating divergent interests without having confrontations and making choices. The relationship of mutual noninterference dampened many of the conflicts which might have erupted with regard to the New

119

Mexico projects. The breach in orderly procedure involved in authorizing Animas–La Plata was not a cause for challenge. It was considered to be a matter between Chairman Aspinall and agencies in the administration; of more general interest, only if progress on the whole basin bill were delayed. The conflict over the division of Gila water was contained among involved parties. Questions as to whether it would be more economical or better for the nation for the water involved to be used by Arizona in its already developed agriculture were never salient. Similarly, most congressmen treated the matter of invasion of the Gila Wilderness as Senator Anderson's affair. In spite of the efforts of conservation groups to make the issue national, it was essentially settled by Senator Anderson himself.

The model indicates and the experience of the case studies confirms that activists who do not share the basic local orientation toward water are extremely difficult to accommodate within the pattern. Mutual noninterference in the cases described here could not contain the conservationist conflict. The basic concerns of conservationists prompt them to interfere in matters affecting the land anywhere. The interests of the conservationists clashed head-on with local supporters of water development through Hooker Dam and could not be satisfied at the same time these local demands were attended to. On the protection of the Gila Wilderness, the conservationists were simply overriden, and their fears were afforded only as much attention as Senator Anderson wished to give them. The result of conservationist opposition on the Grand Canyon dams was to bring the majority-building process to a grinding halt.

Gaps and Shortcomings in the Model

It has been demonstrated that as a description of the major influences in water policy and as an indication of how these factors lead one to another, the model serves very well. However, the model is a better description of how policy happened in water than a thorough analysis of why it happened. What follows are some suggestions for further amplifying and testing the model.

The nature of the localized perceptions of the water issue merits further exploration. Why is it that localized benefits of water development are so much more salient than the long-range implications to the nation? A study of the location, distribution, and intensity of public opinion on water would add important information here, as would a study of opinion formation.

The model identifies locally oriented activists as responding to localized perceptions of benefits in water development. The representative relationship implied here probably has a number of complexities and variations worthy of study. Senators, with broader constituencies, may tend to take a role with regard to water issues that House members are not free to choose. A Congressman Aspinall may have had less flexibility than a Senator Jackson. If this were the case, it would then follow that the state engineer had a role with little flexibility. The specialized constituency of a state engineer or the public which followed his actions prescribed a heavy involvement in water issues. Whatever leeway he could manage to exercise must have been the result of his claim to professional expertise and his skill in the leadership of his water-conscious public.

The recruitment and careers of activists in water policy may have had just as much effect upon how they perceived risks and reward in water development and may have defined their representative function. Where activists had achieved their positions partly because of their record in water and where in the course of their careers they had accumulated the burden of past water battles won and lost, there was a built-in involvement which went beyond the immediate political environment. For instance, it is likely that Chairman Aspinall, given his long career in water politics, would have felt the responsibility to protect Colorado's water however his western slope constituency felt about it. Likewise, it appears probable that the sting of defeat for New Mexico representatives in *Arizona v. California* generated for those involved a justification for reopening the matter of division of water on the Gila outside any concrete demand for new water or firm ideas as to the uses to which it would be put. It would be revealing to contrast the sort of positions which local representatives, more recently recruited to the issue, took in relation to the activists with similar constituencies who had long been involved in the issue.

The model did little to explain or predict the impact of activists in the formulation of opinion on water issues. Undoubtedly the activists acted to reinforce local perceptions, but it would have been useful to know how and to what extent. It is difficult to identify, for example, the extent to which the attachment of State Engineer Reynolds to new water for New Mexico shaped the goals and desires of the New Mexico Interstate Stream Commission and southwestern New Mexicans.

Leverage Points for Change

The pattern of politics described in the model in chapter 3 and generally observed in the case of the Colorado River Basin Act and the role New Mexico played in it form a kind of closed circuit. Local perceptions of water issues led through a series of conduits to water policy which was generally responsive to localized demands. Policy was internally inconsistent and frequently at odds with technical tests of feasibility. It followed no general rationale other than that of political feasibility, of the degree of support generated by particular proposals. This sort of policy tended to reinforce the perceptions of purely localized stakes in water development.

However irrational water policy may have appeared from other points of view, the pattern of policy making in water was politically rational. It was the appropriate response to the risks and rewards presented by the issue. To alter effectively the water policy and the pattern through which it was made, the stakes in the issue had to be altered. At bottom, this meant changing people's perceptions. Water had to be viewed in other than local terms. This presented a gargantuan task of political leadership and policy. In the tight circle where the pattern of politics traced from perceptions to policy, there was little incentive for involved activists to take up such a job.

Within the broad policy-making pattern on water as sketched here, certain weaknesses could be identified which might lead to instabilities and opportunities to alter the pattern. One potential leverage point for change was the distance which sometimes separated expectations and policy. In the process of achieving local unity, various persons and groups came to expect direct and impressive benefits from water development. This was certainly true of the local Hooker Dam and La Plata Project backers. In increasingly diversified localities, not everyone was likely to be satisfied with the outcome. Municipal and industrial users in reclamation projects, for example, consistently paid more and got less. Repeated disappointments could lead to changed perceptions.

Another potential leverage point resulted from the inherent weakness of the consent-building relations in water. As the case of the Grand Canyon dams illustrates, mutual noninterference was not the proper relation to overcome substantial opposition if conflict could not be avoided. It was reasonable to anticipate more conflict on water development in the future. Interests representing competing uses of funds were bound to challenge water development more frequently as budgets got tighter. The strength of preservationists and conservationists was waxing. They were likely to challenge many traditional water projects. The difficulty that some water development proposals were then experiencing was illustrated by the fact that after it was taken up in earnest, it took three Congresses and over five years to pass the Central Arizona Project. Because the existing pattern of politics got chronically bogged down in creating consent, dissatisfaction led to changed perceptions and an altered pattern.

Changes in perceptions of water were then occurring in response to happenings and events outside the pattern. The use of land, air, and water, and the connection of all three had become salient to persons and groups who had not had a previous stake in water development. At the point where the natural world makes water a national issue, a different pattern of politics could emerge.

9

Afterword on the Implementation of the Colorado River Basin Projects Act

Introduction

The Colorado River Basin Act was repeatedly modified during the legislative process to accommodate different interests whose support or lack of opposition was crucial to passage by Congress. As chapter 8 concluded, political feasibilities determined the design of the policy. The influence of politics does not abate when bills are signed into law. Modifications of laws made during implementation are often accommodations to shifting events, attitudes, and influences. Not one of the projects discussed in the body of this book has been completed even though the law which authorized them is over twenty years old. Given the opportunity this long period of time has provided for shifts of influence to take place, it is not at all surprising that profound changes have been made.

The following chronologies of key changes in the Central Arizona Project, Animas–La Plata Project, and Hooker Dam sketch the broad outlines of the policy designs emerging from implementation. What is presented is no more than an overview, without the in-depth research that informed the original case study. The intention is to satisfy the reader's likely curiosity about what has happened. Further, the chronologies provide the basis for a final examination of change and continuity as exemplified in these key projects.

The Central Arizona Project: Chronology of the Redesign

1977—Advance planning, preparation of Environmental Impact Statements and construction of the Navajo Generating Station necessary to provide energy for project pumping delays beginning work on the aqueduct construction until 1976. Less than one year later, President Carter places the entire project in jeopardy with his famous "hit list." Once again internal differences are set aside and Arizonans form a united front in support of the CAP with the governor, members of Congress, and interest group leaders joining in a campaign to save the project. The major newspapers of the state roundly criticize the president's actions as rash and ill founded.[1]

While most major interests in Arizona remain steadfastly supportive, the restudy of the project ordered by the president provides an opportunity and forums in which to criticize and suggest modifications to the project. While carefully expressing their support for the project as a whole, several central Arizona Indian tribes demand more project water go to their reservations. Orme Dam, a regulating and flood-control reservoir planned at the confluence of the Salt and Verde rivers is opposed by the Indians because it would inundate a section of the Fort McDowell Reservation. Environmentalists also object to Orme Dam because of its destructive impact upon wildlife habitat and natural areas.[2]

Following the reanalysis, President Carter announces that construction will proceed on the CAP, but with the elimination of Orme Dam. Since the 1968 authorizing legislation provided for Orme or a suitable alternative, and the president did not preclude alternatives to the dam, an inter-agency task force sets out to find an acceptable alternative. The president also recommends that future federal funding for the CAP be contingent upon further studies of groundwater supplies and improved state groundwater management. In announcing his decision to continue construction of the CAP, the only favorable factor the president mentions is the allocation of project water to Indians.[3]

1980—Following increasing pressures from the Carter administration to adopt groundwater reform and settle outstanding Indian water disputes, Arizona turns its attention to reforming the water code. In a Phoenix speech, Secretary of Interior Andrus warns that the state needs to act swiftly and decisively if it hopes to avoid the loss of influence with the secretary who has authority to make final decisions about allocations of CAP water.[4] The Arizona Groundwater Management Act of 1980 is hammered out after months of negotiations among the major water interests in the state. A strong personal effort by Governor Bruce Babbitt keeps negotiations alive when vociferous opposition from the agricultural community threatens to stall the agreement. The new code represents the end of the laissez-faire approach Arizona has long taken to groundwater and a basic shift of influence away from agriculture and in favor of the cities and mines. The goal of no overdraft of aquifers is to be met by the year 2025, and every category of water user is to be subjected to periodically established conservation requirements. CAP water, where it is available, is to be substituted for groundwater used in agriculture. The code contains provisions to retire agricultural lands after a specific time if it becomes necessary in order to eliminate overdraft. New residential developments are required to prove a 100-year assured supply of water.

Indian tribes do not participate in the negotiations of the new groundwater code and Indian water rights are not addressed by it. Tentatively recommended allocations of CAP water by Secretary Andrus provides substantially enlarged Indian supplies which are protected against shortages by a priority ahead of non-Indian agriculture.

1983—The Southern Arizona Water Rights Settlement Act (SAWRSA) becomes law and provides CAP water to the Tohono O'Odham tribe south of Tucson and insures construction of the Tucson aqueduct. The act relieves many of the previous concerns of Tucson leaders about security of water supply. Without the assurance of CAP water the city had no prospect of eliminating the overdraft as required by the Arizona Groundwater Management Act. It was feared that once CAP water reached Phoenix, Tucson would not have the political clout to bring it the additional 100 miles south. Further, groundwater supplies to the city were threatened by a Tohono O'Odham lawsuit aimed at stopping the city wells from drawing water out from under the reservation as it had been doing since the 1930s.[5] The lawsuit is abandoned in SAWRSA.

The Southern Arizona Water Rights Settlement Act clearly benefits Tucson, is a mixed blessing to the Tohono O'Odham tribe, and is expensive for the federal government. The Indians receive wet water instead of paper water rights, but agree to limit their own underground pumping and to accept part of their water allocation in effluent.[6]

1984—Plan 6 is approved by Interior Secretary William Clarke as a suitable alternative to Orme Dam. The plan includes three construction projects: Cliff Dam on the Verde River, raised Roosevelt Dam on the Salt River, and a rebuilt Waddell Dam on the Agua Fria River. Plan 6 is backed by a coalition of cities, utilities, and urban real estate developers. Major floods in Phoenix in the 1978–80 period created a demand for greater flood protection which could be provided by Cliff Dam. Further, flood control would permit a billion-dollar development along the Salt River—called the Rio Salado—with bike paths, resorts, marinas, museums, and lakes. New safety standards for dams adopted by the Army Corps of Engineers brand existing facilities on the Salt, Verde, and Agua Fria rivers substandard. This together with dam safety legislation providing federal funding for upgrading substandard dams raises a financing opportunity. Flood control funds could defray part of the cost of facilities which are ten times as costly as the original Orme Dam. However, Senator Howard Metzenbaum vows to filibuster if dam safety funds are diverted to build a new dam such as Cliff.[7] Only a few days after the approval of Plan 6, bald eagles' nests are found in the path of the proposed Cliff Dam.

1985—A coalition of national environmental groups files a lawsuit claiming that Cliff Dam would destroy bald eagle foraging areas and a ten-mile stretch of wild and scenic river through the Sonoran Desert. However, the U.S. Fish and Wildlife Service issues a biological opinion that Cliff Dam will not jeopardize endangered bald eagles if strict guidelines are followed.

1986—Arizona cities and water districts sign a cost-sharing agreement with the secretary of interior. On the Arizonans' part, the objectives are to enhance chances that Plan 6 will be undertaken, to reduce the overall construction schedule for the CAP, and to avoid exceeding the authorized cost ceiling for the CAP.[8] A central goal of the Reagan administration is to force local beneficiaries to pay a larger share of costs in order to ease the strain on federal budgets. Arizonans agree to pay $348 million of Plan 6's $1.1 billion cost in advance in exchange for the federal government's promise to speed completion of the CAP.

The agreement attests to the resilience of the united front and the successful resolution of numbers of intrastate disagreements about appropriate allocations of costs. In coming to an agreement, rifts are patched between the congressional delegation, Governor Bruce Babbitt, the Central Arizona Water Conservation District Board set up to manage the CAP, the Salt River Project, and the city of Tucson (which felt that Phoenix should pay for benefits of Plan 6).[9]

1987—U.S. General Accounting Office concludes that the CAP's updated cost, $3.32 billion, exceeds authorized spending limits, and questions whether Plan 6 is legally an alternative to Orme Dam or must be authorized again by the current Congress. The environmental coalition against Orme Dam gains strength in Congress. The delegation is concerned about the potential loss of funding for the entire Plan 6 if a House floor amendment is offered to the water and power 1988 funding as threatened by environmentally oriented Congressman Lawrence Coughlin (R-Pa.). Udall tells a press conference, "There was an indication that we were in trouble. We did some quick head counting and it was obvious we did not have the votes we had in the past. Each year you are a little weaker. They are a little stronger."[10]

After three days of closed-meeting negotiations with environmentalists, Arizona declares the controversial Cliff Dam dead. In exchange, environmentalists agree to accept Plan 6 as the legitimate alternative to Orme Dam, and not to oppose funding for the remaining parts of Plan 6. Congress appropriates $237.1 million, a record annual outlay in support of the CAP minus Cliff Dam.

1989—Tucson aqueduct construction approaches completion scheduled for 1991. Even before deliveries begin, it is clear that Colorado River water will not eliminate the overdraft of the groundwater table. Cities in Active Management Areas designated by the Arizona Groundwater Management Act look for other sources to provide an assured 100-year water supply as required by law. The groundwater in La Paz County in the southwestern part of Arizona becomes an obvious target source of additional water for cities in the Phoenix area because the CAP canal passing through the rural county provides a conduit for water transfers. The city of Tucson begins negotiations with Tohono O'Odham for lease of CAP water gained through SAWRSA. Similar negotiations take place between the federal government, Phoenix, and the Salt River/Pima Maricopa Indian community. While these negotiations do not involve stretching a new concrete trail such as the CAP is laying across the desert, the purpose of providing water to serve growth is the same.

The Animas–La Plata Project: Chronology of Redesign

1970—An important congressional watchdog to insure concurrent construction of the Central Arizona Project and the five Colorado projects is eliminated. After redistricting diminishes the number of supporters within his constiuency, Wayne Aspinall is defeated in a reelection bid.

1984—Of the five Colorado water projects authorized in the Colorado River Basin Projects Act, construction so far has begun on only two, Dallas Creek Dam and the Dolores Project. The Animas–La Plata is not included in President Reagan's budget. In Farmington, New Mexico, a prospective beneficiary of the Animas–La Plata, the city council authorizes its attorney to investigate legal action to force the federal government to stop work on the CAP because California and Arizona are now getting "our water free."[11]

Prominent politicians and administrators warn that the Animas–La Plata Project has little chance of success without up-front money from the states of Colorado and New Mexico. A long-term Durango rancher and project supporter who had testified in its favor eighteen years earlier complained, "The cost-sharing proposal means the federal government is reneging on promises made in 1968 when the Animas was authorized by Congress, that it would be built with Federal revenues from hydroelectric generating plants in the Colorado River Basin."[12]

A second substantial impediment to the construction of Animas–La Plata is the lack of agreement on Indian water rights. The project area has about 1,600 Ute Mountain Utes and about 1,000 Southern Utes. The town of Towaoc in extreme southwestern Colorado and headquarters of the Ute Mountain Ute tribe has no pipeline and must truck in water daily. While it is possible that some Indian needs can be served by the Dolores Project under construction, Animas–La Plata provides a means to satisfy reserved rights claims. Indians are suing on the basis of these rights in Colorado state courts and, if upheld, will carry a priority date of 1868, making them by far the most senior water rights in the region. Existing rights of non-Indian farmers, ranchers, and towns would be jeopardized. Local residents believe the burden should be shouldered by the federal government, since it has trust responsibility, rather than themselves.

A third impediment is getting continual funding. Obtaining construction money each year is a "brutal exercise" for the Colorado congressional delegation.[13] Project supporters regret that the municipal recipients of project water are places like Durango and Cortez rather than cities with real political clout like Phoenix and Tucson which are effectively pressuring for the CAP.

1985—Congressman Mike Strange (R-Colo.) succeeds in obtaining start-up funds for Animas–La Plata in the supplemental fiscal year 1985 appropriations. Project sponsors promise that a cost-sharing agreement will be worked out with the federal government before the money is actually spent. A June 30, 1986, deadline for negotiations is set.[14]

1986—A local cost-sharing agreement acceptable to the Office of Management and Budget (OMB) and other parties is negotiated. Colorado agrees to put up $69 million in cash contribution toward construction of the project, $11 million for the Indian development fund, and to defer $139 million in phased construction of irrigated acreage. New Mexico agrees to defer irrigation of 1,900 acres and the San Juan Water Commission of San Juan County, New Mexico, agrees to pay $12 million, its full share of construction costs, during construction of the facilities needed for municipal and industrial water supply. The federal government agrees to put up $359,400,000 for construction of what is likely to be a scaled-down project. The agreement is described as a win for all parties by a spokesperson of the Department of Interior.

OMB is a reluctant partner, and would not have signed on had it not been for the advantages of settling the Indian water rights dispute and pressure from the congressional delegation. Senators Pete Domenici (R-N.Mex.), William Armstrong (R-Colo.), and Congressman Michael L. Strange (R-Colo.) are said to have ordered OMB director James C. Miller III to Capitol Hill to tell him, "Water is not only in short supply in the West particularly in the San Juan Basin, but it is a religion." Senator Domenici is in a good position to exercise influence with the administration because he is chairman of the Senate Budget Committee.[15]

Opponents of the project range from spending-conscious officials and fiscal conservatives to no-growthers, environmentalists, and rafters in southwestern Colorado. They contend the project would ruin the Animas River, create a boom and bust during and after construction, and provide water that would be expensive for debt-ridden farmers. Taxpayers for the Animas–La Plata Referendum, a Durango-based group, contend that an all-Indian project would be cheaper. Project supporters and the Southern Ute tribe say that an Indian-only project would not fly politically, nor should it because Indians would be left out in the future. The Interior Department makes a try at dealing separately with the Indian tribes but is rejected. Indians say that they will not be bought off with money when what they really want is water.[16]

1987—Representative Morris Udall (D-Az.) elects to handle the Indian water rights settlement related to Animas–La Plata in the full committee of the House Interior Committee rather than refer it to the less favorable forum of the Water and Power Resources Subcommittee. Udall has been successful in settling four Indian water rights disputes.

Voters support the Animas–La Plata Project on a referendum on project repayment forced to a vote by project opponents. The project gets 59 percent of the total vote in favor of an arrangement providing Durango area taxpayers share $7.3 million of the $380 million project.

1988—President Reagan signs Indian water rights settlement legislation for Colorado's Ute tribes after a conflict-ridden course through Congress. During a bitter battle in the Senate, William Armstrong (R-Colo.) compromises with several western Republican senators who were concerned that the Indians' proposed off-reservation use of their water, such as leasing to California, might set a precedent of interstate transfers of federal reserve water rights. The compromise language provides that the Indians will receive a federal reserve water right for water used on the reservations. If water is to be leased off reservation, the federal right would be relinquished and the Indians forced to comply with Colorado state water rights and the law of the river. While satisfying western water interests, this language arouses the opposition of Senator Bill Bradley (D-N.J.) who contends that Indian interests are not being served and also objects on environmental grounds. Bradley is mollified by a resolution limiting the off-reservation-leasing language specifically to the two Colorado tribes.[17]

The settlement calls for various state and local entities to pay 38 percent of the project's estimated $380 million cost for the first phase, which is the highest percentage of local cost sharing so far in the history of reclamation. Even with the generous local cost share, the project still faces the annual appropriations battle. The House Appropriations Committee approves $1.9 million for 1989, far less than the $7.8 million requested to keep the project on its twelve-year construction schedule.

Hooker Dam Project: Chronology of Redesign

1973—The Hooker Dam's most influential champion, Senator Clinton Anderson, retires from Congress.

1977—Hooker Dam appears on Carter "hit list" and a restudy takes place during which environmentalists voice their long-standing objections. The restudy concludes that the original concept of the spillway over the dam was flawed. Costs of the project have risen since 1968, undermining economic feasibility. Hooker Dam is eliminated, but the president's task force does not preclude consideration of the alternative to Hooker Dam at the Connor site.

1982—The Bureau of Reclamation recommends alternative Connor Dam site.

1983—State of New Mexico agrees to share $300,000 of the costs of the Bureau of Reclamation feasibility study of the Connor alternative.

1986—United States Fish and Wildlife Service announces that the habitat of the loach and spikedace minnows, which are endangered species, would be damaged by a dam at the Connor site. A final designation of habitat is postponed due to the urging of New Mexico water officials. Even without the minnows' listings as endangered species, the proposed Connor Dam is plagued with problems including:

The dam must be paid for. An Audubon Society newsletter notes that the federal government is no longer footing most of the bill for projects, and the cost to Silver City might be as much as $7.5 million per year for twenty years plus a lesser amount for the next ten years.

A contract has to be signed with Arizona's San Carlos Irrigation Drainage District, which will be exchanging water with New Mexico.

A court approval is needed to modify the Gila decree which regulates water use on the Gila River.[18]

The accumulated difficulties prompt local residents and some state officials to search for alternatives. Groundwater pumping to supply Silver City rather than relying on surface water impoundments is one alternative suggested. In addition, the Bureau of Reclamation begins to explore a smaller dam site in Schoolhouse Canyon. A spokesperson for the Hooker Dam Association objects, stating that no downstream flood control would be provided at the smaller site, and so Arizonans will neither support nor help to pay for the dam. Further, the small dam would not capture all of the 18,000 acre-feet per year acquired from Arizona on the Gila River in the Colorado River Basin Act.[19]

1988—In a bid to keep the project alive, the New Mexico Game and Fish Commission votes three to two that the state can have a dam on the Gila River. Members of the commission agree to look for ways to preserve the spikedace and loach minnows if and when the proposed Connor Dam is built.[20] In spite of the delays and remaining hurdles to construction at the Connor site, New Mexico State Engineer Steve Reynolds remarks, "Sooner or later it has to come. This project is the only perpetual supply of water for the Silver City area. It is far from dead."[21]

Examples of Change and Continuity

Parts of the model of policy making set out in chapter 3 fit rather poorly the patterns of influence at work in the twenty-year implementation process. For instance, the president and his staff arm, the Office of Management and Budget, have become stronger sources of influence. Instead of being relatively uninvolved in water development, President Jimmy Carter actively opposed construction programs. Placing the Central Arizona Project and Hooker Dam on the "hit list" for discontinued funding had much more profound effects than previous presidents had tried to achieve in water matters. The Reagan administration was more positive about water development but reluctant to spend federal funds for it. New cost-sharing arrangements basically changed the benefits flowing from federal water projects as illustrated in the CAP and Animas–La Plata Project. That the beneficiaries should pay more of the costs was a great achievement for the budget conscious, especially at OMB. At the same time, OMB's influence over the Animas–La Plata Project had clear limits similar to those faced by its predecessor, the Bureau of the Budget. OMB, like BOB, was forced to give approval on the basis of politics rather than economic analysis. In the OMB's case, the rationale was the federal government's trust obligation to Indians rather than the power of Congressman Aspinall.

Arenas in the pattern of policy making have shifted somewhat from the federal to the state and local levels. State action was required to pass the groundwater reforms essential to get the secretary of interior's go-ahead for the CAP. In both Arizona and Colorado, states and localities were involved in approving cost-sharing arrangements. Congress has continued to be a significant arena because these are federal projects requiring some federal funding. At the same time, the role of members of Congress in water policy has been altered.

The underpinnings to the rules of mutual accommodation and mutual noninterference that operated in 1968 have been eroded. In an era of budget stringency, it did not appear reasonable to legislators to vote for water development outside their own constituency area when there was a low probability that the favor could ever be returned. Western water projects became the focus of attack for some eastern and midwestern members of Congress who complained of regional favoritism and inefficiency. The threat of a floor challenge to Plan 6 of the CAP and the opposition of Senator Bill Bradley to Animas–La Plata are exemplary of the extent to which the consent-building relations have changed.

Amid these changes, the constants set out in the first chapter are clearly evident. The impetus and support for these projects has continued to emanate from local interests with strong stakes in the growth and development they believe will be fostered by projects. Threats to the CAP caused Arizona interests to close ranks in opposition to Carter's reform strategy. When given an opportunity in a referendum, the people in southern Colorado rallied around the Animas–La Plata Project, believing that even if they were forced to pay a substantial part of the cost, the area as a whole would benefit. After years of disappointment, the Hooker Dam Association in Silver City continued to pressure officials for action. The belief in the Midas touch of water persists.

The chronologies provide evidence that water politics is less closed today than it was in 1968. There is a clear shift in influence with previously underrepresented groups such as Indians and environmentalists playing a larger role in negotiations than they did in the 1960s. In the less hospitable political environment for water projects, the support of previously marginal groups is now essential for successful coalition building.

The Animas–La Plata Project would never have been able to jump the administrative and congressional hurdles had it not been "riding the Indian pony." It is an interesting twist that provisions favoring Indian irrigation were eliminated from the project in 1966 in order to improve the benefit/cost ratio. In 1986, the provisions favoring Indians protected the project from opposition by OMB and members of Congress. Similarly, it is unlikely that the Tucson aqueduct would ever have been completed had it not been a necessary part of an Indian water rights settlement.

Having determined that decision making is somewhat more open, it must also be concluded that neither the CAP nor Animas–La Plata has been so modified as to really satisfy equity concerns. In both cases, Indians were served because non-Indian interests were also substantially benefited. Indians did not frame the agenda, and what they got from legislation was very different from what they would have asked had their needs and desires been of central concern. Indeed, one of Senator Bill Bradley's strongest points was that Animas–La Plata was a poor precedent for helping Indians.

Environmentalists have also come to wield life-and-death power over some water projects. Their opposition was the death knell for Cliff Dam in the CAP, and their support of endangered species laws contributes to blocking Connor Dam. While some environmental insults have been removed from projects, the resulting policies fall considerably short of insuring environmentally sensitive water management.

There continue to be substantial environmental and other costs of water policies that are not well recognized and that are being largely passed on to the future. The Colorado River is overallocated, and millions of people are being attracted to the urban Southwest on the basis of water supplies of uncertain quality and quantity. Global climate change threatens hotter and drier weather, which will heighten uncertainties and conflict. Water policy is continuing to be largely unresponsive to ecological limits inherent in desert environments.

Notes

Chapter 1

1. Speech before University of Arizona students and faculty by Morris K. and Stewart Udall, 1987.

2. William E. Martin, Helen M. Ingram, and Nancy K. Laney, "A Willingness to Play: Analysis of Water Resources Development," in *Western Journal of Agricultural Economics* (July 1982): 135.

3. F. Lee Brown and Helen M. Ingram, *Water and Poverty in the Southwest* (Tucson: University of Arizona Press, 1987), 36.

4. Susan Christopher Nunn and Helen M. Ingram, "Information, the Decision Forum, and Third Party Effects of Water Transfers," *Water Resources Research* (Spring 1988).

5. William E. Martin, Helen M. Ingram, Dennis C. Cory, and Mary G. Wallace, "Toward Sustaining a Desert Metropolis: Water and Land Use in Tucson, Arizona" in M. T. El Ashly and D.C. Gibbons (eds.), *Water and the Arid Lands of the United States* (London: Cambridge University Press, 1988).

6. Arthur Maass and Raymond L. Anderson, . . . *and the Desert Shall Rejoice* (Cambridge: MIT Press, 1978), 4.

7. Yehezkel Dror, *Public Policy Reexamined* (San Francisco: Chandler Publishing Co., 1968).

8. "Water and Choice in the Colorado Basin: An Example of Alternatives in Water Management." A report by the Committee on Water of the National Research Council, Gilbert F. White, chairman (Washington, D.C.: National Academy of Sciences, 1968).

9. Donald Worster, *Rivers of Empire: Water, Aridity and Growth in the American West* (New York: Pantheon Books, 1985).

10. Daniel McCool, *Command of the Waters: Iron Triangles, Federal Water Development, and Indian Water* (Berkeley: University of California Press, 1987), 6.

11. Philip L. Fradkin, *A River No More* (Tucson: University of Arizona Press, 1981), 154.

12. Robert Gottlieb, *A Life of Its Own: The Politics and Power of Water* (December 1987). In press.

13. W. E. Martin, et al., "Toward Sustaining a Desert Metropolis."

14. Theodore J. Lowi, "American Business, Public Policy, Case Studies and Political Theory," *World Politics*, Vol. 16, No. 4 (July 1964).

15. William L. Kahrl, *Water and Power* (Berkeley: University of California Press, 1982).

16. Helen M. Ingram, "Politics of Water Allocation" in Dean F. Peterson and

A. Barry Crawford (eds.), *Values and Choices in the Development of the Colorado River Basin* (Tucson: University of Arizona Press, 1978), 61–75.

17. Worster, *Rivers of Empire*.

18. McCool, *Command of the Waters*, 21.

19. J. N. Clarke and D. McCool, *Staking Out the Terrain* (Albany: State University of New York Press, 1985).

20. Marc Reisner, *Cadillac Desert* (New York: Viking, 1986), 248.

21. Helen M. Ingram, "The Changing Decision Rules in the Politics of Water Development," *Water Resources Bulletin*, Vol. 8, No. 6 (December 8, 1972): 1181.

22. Dean Mann, "Political Incentives in U.S. Water Policy: Relationships Between Distributive and Regulatory Politics," in Matthew Holden and Dennis L. Dresang (eds.), *What Government Does* (Beverly Hills, Calif.: Sage Publications, 1975), 94–123.

23. Charles Du Mars and Helen M. Ingram, "Congressional Quantification of Indian Reserved Water Rights: A Definitive Solution or a Mirage?" *Natural Resources Journal*, Vol. 20, No. 1 (January 1980): 17–43.

24. Daniel McCool, Monroe E. Price, and Gary D. Weatherford, "Indian Water Rights in Theory and Practice: Navajo Experience in the Colorado River Basin," *Law and Contemporary Problems* (Winter 1976).

25. Arthur Maass, *Muddy Waters: The Army Engineers and the Nation's Rivers* (Cambridge: Harvard University Press, 1951).

26. Frank Gregg, "Irrelevance and Innovation in Water Policy: A Baseline for the Future." Paper presented at the American Water Resources Association annual meeting, Salt Lake City, 1987. Gregg was chairman of the New England River Basin Commission and observer to the U.S. Water Resources Council from 1967 to 1978.

27. Hanna J. Cortner and Joe Auburg, "Water Resources Policy: Old Models and New Realities." Paper presented at the annual meeting of the Western Political Science Association, San Francisco, March 9–13, 1988.

28. Daniel McCool, "Using Measures of Budgetary Success to Evaluate Subgovernment Theory: The Case of Federal Water Resource Development." Paper presented at the annual meeting of the Western Political Science Association, San Francisco, March 9–13, 1988.

29. Hanna J. Cortner, "The Water Resources Development Act of 1986: A Non-Federal Perspective." Paper presented at the annual meeting of the Western Political Science Association, San Francisco, March 9–13, 1988.

30. Maurice M. Kelso, William E. Martin, and Lawrence E. Mack, *Water Supplies and Economic Growth in an Arid Environment: An Arizona Case Study* (Tucson: University of Arizona Press, 1972), 455–56.

31. In recent years a movement, termed New Resource Economics, has provided a more strident version of this same message. See, for example, Terry Anderson, *Water Crisis: Ending the Policy Drought* (Baltimore, Md.: Johns Hopkins Press, 1983).

32. Tony Davis, "State No Longer Chasing New Water Supplies," *Tucson Citizen*, January 10, 1985.

33. William E. Martin and Helen M. Ingram, *Planning for Growth in the Southwest* (Washington, D.C.: National Planning Association, 1985).

34. See for example Water Market Update.

35. Gottlieb, *A Life of Its Own*, chapter 1.

36. See *Sporhase v. Nebraska*, 81 U.S. 513 (1982).

37. Lowi, "American Business, Public Policy, Case Studies, and Political Theory."
38. Tim DeYoung and Hank Jenkins-Smith, *Privatizing Water Management: The Hollow Promise of Private Markets*, April 1987. Unpublished paper.
39. Letter from Sullivan realtors to Arizona Department of Water Resources, September 15, 1987. Files.
40. Telephone interview, Edward Osann, National Wildlife Federation, August 17, 1988.
41. Nunn and Ingram, "Third Party Effects of Water Transfers," Water Resources Research.
42. Ibid.
43. Brown and Ingram, *Water and Poverty in the Southwest*.
44. Ibid.
45. Steven Mumme and Helen M. Ingram, "Community Values in Southwestern Water Management," *Policy Studies Review*, Vol. 5, No. 2 (1985): 365–81.
46. Arthur Maass and Myron Fiering, "Civil Works Externalities Assessment." Unpublished paper prepared for the U.S. Army Corps of Engineers Strategic Planning Integration Group, Washington, D.C., 1987.
47. Cortner and Auburg, "Water Resources Policy."
48. Ibid.
49. John Bartlett, *Bartlett's Familiar Quotations*, 628.
50. Martin, et al., "Toward Sustaining a Desert Metropolis: Water and Land Use in Tucson, Arizona."

Chapter 2

1. *Pacific Southwest Water Plan*, Bureau of Reclamation report, United States Department of the Interior, January 1964.
2. *Animas–La Plata Project, Colorado and New Mexico*, letter from the secretary of the interior transmitting a report on the Animas–La Plata Project, pursuant to the provisions of 58 Stat. 1187 (Washington, D.C.: U.S. Government Printing Office, 1966).
3. *Lower Colorado River Basin Project*, hearing before the Subcommittee of Irrigation and Reclamation of the Committee on Interior and Insular Affairs, House of Representatives, Eighty-ninth Congress, First Session, 1965, 150.
4. *Colorado River Basin Project*, hearings, ibid., Ninetieth Congress, Second Session, 1968, 825.
5. *Animas–La Plata Project*, vi.
6. S. E. Reynolds, *Twenty-eighth Biennial Report of the State Engineer of New Mexico*, July 1, 1966, to June 30, 1968, 54.
7. Ralph K. Huitt, "Political Feasibility," *Political Science and Public Policy*, ed. by Austin Ranney (Chicago: Markham Publishing Company, 1968), 266.

Chapter 3

1. Theodore J. Lowi, "Distribution, Regulation, Redistribution: The Functions of Government," *Public Policies and Their Politics*, ed. by Randall B. Ripley (New York: W. W. Norton and Company, 1966), 27.
2. The general conceptual model of policy making relied on here was synthesized from a number of different students and diverse approaches to the subject. Principal contributors include Theodore Lowi, Aaron Wildavsky, Charles E. Lind-

blom, and Charles O. Jones.

3. Anticipation of boomtown prosperity from Echo Park's construction was part of the motive for the vocal and adamant backing for the project forthcoming from Vernal, Utah.

Owen Stratton and Philip Sirotkin, *The Echo Park Controversy* (Tuscaloosa: University of Alabama Press, 1959).

4. David Braybrooke and Charles E. Lindblom note in *A Strategy of Decision: Policy Evaluation as a Social Process* (New York: The Free Press, 1963), 56, that when the focus of attention is upon means in policy analysis, there can be no examination of alternate policies to reach agreed-upon objectives.

5. Kenneth J. Gergen has developed a three-dimensional model of activism or leverage in public policy which includes the relevance of the issue, the sense of personal efficacy, and the resources at various stages of the policy process.

"Assessing the Leverage Points in the Process of Policy Formation," *The Study of Policy Formation*, ed. by Raymond A. Bauer and Kenneth J. Gergen (New York: The Free Press, 1968), 165.

6. Norman Wengert, "The Politics of River Basin Development," *Law and Contemporary Problems* 22 (1957): 258, 263 particularly.

7. Arthur Maass, *Muddy Waters: The Army Engineers and the Nation's Rivers* (Cambridge: Harvard University Press, 1951), 24.

8. Stratton and Sirotkin, 11–12.

9. Samuel P. Huntington notes in "Congressional Response to the Twentieth Century," *The Congress and America's Future*, ed. by David B. Truman (Englewood Cliffs, N.J.: Prentice-Hall, 1965), 13, that in 1963, 70 percent of congressional leaders were still living in the place of their birth.

10. H. Douglas Price, "The Electoral Arena," ibid., 50.

11. Richard Neustadt, *Presidential Power: The Politics of Leadership* (New York: John Wiley and Sons, 1960).

12. Data compiled from *Congressional Directories*, Eightieth Congress, 1947–48, through the Ninetieth Congress, 1967–68.

13. Donald R. Matthews, *U.S. Senators and Their World* (Chapel Hill: University of North Carolina Press, 1960), 95–96.

Charles L. Clapp, *The Congressman: His Work as He Sees It* (Garden City: Anchor Books, 1963), 123–26.

14. Neustadt, 22 ff.

15. Lowi, 30.

16. Matthews, chapter 5; Clapp, chapter 1.

17. Henry Hart, "Crisis, Community, and Consent in Water Politics," *Law and Contemporary Problems* 22 (1957): 510–35.

18. Aaron Wildavsky, "The Political Economy of Efficiency: Cost Benefit Analysis, Systems Analysis, and Program Budgeting," *Political Science and Public Policy*, ed. by Austin Ranney (Chicago: Markham Publishing Company, 1968), 64.

19. Herbert Marshall, "Politics and Efficiency in Water Development," *Water Research*, ed. by Allen Kneese and Stephen Smith (Resources for the Future: Johns Hopkins Press, 1965), 294.

20. Stratton and Sirotkin, 9–10.

21. Wildavsky, 64.

22. Wengert, 263.

Chapter 4

1. Interview with Morris K. Udall, May 26, 1969.
2. Ernest A. Englebert, *Policy Issues of the Pacific Southwest Water Plan* (Boulder: University of Colorado Press, 1965), 129–35.
3. Udall interview.
4. Survey of the news on the CAP, *Arizona Daily Star* and *Phoenix Republic,* 1965–68.
5. *Arizona Daily Star* editorials, March 18 and March 24, 1967.
6. *Lower Colorado River Basin Project,* hearing before the Subcommittee on Irrigation and Reclamation of the Committee on Interior and Insular Affairs, House of Representatives, Eighty-ninth Congress, First Session, 1965, 846.
7. Ibid., 846–47.
8. Udall interview.
9. Dean E. Mann, *The Politics of Water in Arizona* (Tucson: The University of Arizona Press, 1963), 131.
10. *Twenty-first Annual Report of the Arizona Interstate Stream Commission,* July 1, 1967, to June 30, 1968.
11. Mann, 128.
12. Englebert, 131.
13. *Central Arizona Project,* hearings before the Subcommittee on Water and Power Resources of the Committee on Interior and Insular Affairs, United States Senate, Ninetieth Congress, First Session, 1967, 146.
14. Owen Stratton and Phillip Sirotkin, *The Echo Park Controversy* (Tuscaloosa: University of Alabama Press, 1959), 9.
15. Morris K. Udall files on the Central Arizona Project, memorandum from Udall to Rhodes, September 22, 1966, Special Collections, University of Arizona Library, Tucson, Arizona.
16. M. K. U. files, Wayne Aspinall quoted in a joint statement by Udall and Rhodes, September 1966.
17. Interview with Sterling Munro, administrative assistant to Senator Jackson, May 26, 1969.
18. Interview with Jerry T. Verkler, staff director, Senate Committee on Interior and Insular Affairs, May 22, 1969.
19. Udall interview.
20. *New York Times,* July 25, 1966.
21. Interview with Thomas Foley, congressman from Washington, May 22, 1969.
22. M. K. U. files, memorandum from Udall to Rhodes.
23. M. K. U. files, Udall-Rhodes joint statement.
24. *Congressional Quarterly,* "Colorado River Bill," November 1, 1968, 3019.
25. Foley interview.
26. Ibid.
27. M. K. U. files, tally book.
28. M. K. U. files, memorandum from Udall to Rhodes.
29. Ibid.
30. Daniel A. Dreyfus, "The Colorado River Basin Project: Evolution of a Project Plan." Unpublished statement presented before the Seminar on Water Sciences and Management, Johns Hopkins University, Baltimore, Maryland, February 5, 1969.
31. Governor Reagan quoted in the *Twenty-first Annual Report* of the AISC.

32. *Congressional Record,* August 7, 1967, S11050.
33. *Twenty-first Annual Report* of the AISC.
34. M. K. U. files, Udall memorandum for the files, August 10, 1967.
35. M. K. U. files, letter from Udall to McCormack, August 11, 1967.
36. Ibid.
37. M. K. U. files, letters from Aspinall to Colorado governor John Love, October 1967.
38. Udall, "Town Hall Speech," December 19, 1967, excerpts from *Congressman's Report* on the CAP, VII, No. 1, January 15, 1968.

Chapter 5

1. *Lower Colorado River Basin Project,* hearings before the Subcommittee on Irrigation and Reclamation of the Committee on Interior and Insular Affairs, House of Representatives, Eighty-ninth Congress, Second Session, 1966, 1235.
2. Ibid., 1231.
3. Ibid., 1232.
4. Ibid., 1231.
5. Ibid., 1240.
6. Ibid., 1217.
7. *Animas–La Plata Project, Colorado and New Mexico,* letter from the secretary of the interior transmitting a report on the Animas–La Plata Project, pursuant to the provisions of 58 Stat. 1187 (Washington, D.C.: U.S. Government Printing Office, 1966), 155.
8. Ibid., "Report of the Commissioner of Reclamation," xii.
9. Ibid., "Comments of the Resources Agency of California," 270.
10. Ibid., "Report of the Commissioner of Reclamation," 49.
11. Ibid., "Comments of the State of New Mexico," 276.
12. S. E. Reynolds, "Introduction," *Twenty-sixth Biennial Report of the State Engineer of New Mexico,* July 1, 1962, to June 30, 1964.
13. Interview with S. E. Reynolds, May 8, 1969.
14. Reynolds, *Twenty-sixth Biennial Report,* 119.
15. Interview with David Hale, New Mexico Interstate Stream Commission, Interstate Stream Engineer, June 5, 1969.
16. Interview with Wayne Aspinall, May 26, 1969.
17. Morris K. Udall files on the Central Arizona Project, Colorado River Water Supply, memorandum prepared at the request of the governors, August 13, 1969.
18. M. K. U. files, letter from Rhodes and Udall to Aspinall, June 9, 1965.
19. *Lower Colorado River Basin Project,* hearing, ibid., Eighty-ninth Congress, First Session, 1965, 513.
20. Ibid., 516.
21. Grand Junction (Colo.) *Daily Sentinel,* March 28, 1966.
22. Aspinall interview.
23. Interview with Daniel Dreyfus, professional staff member, Senate Interior and Insular Affairs Committee, 1966 worker in the Budget and Planning Office of the Bureau of Reclamation, May 23, 1969.
24. *Rocky Mountain News,* March 3, 1966.
25. *Animas–La Plata Project,* "Comments of the Bureau of the Budget," vi.
26. Farmington (N.Mex.) *Daily Times,* March 16, 1966, and Grand Junction *Daily*

Sentinel, February 22, 1966.

27. Ibid.

28. Grand Junction *Daily Sentinel*, February 27, 1966.

29. Dreyfus interview.

30. Grand Junction *Daily Sentinel*, March 11, 1966.

31. Response to May 15, 1966, questionnaire, Floyd G. Davis, mayor of Farmington, N.Mex.

32. Farmington *Daily Times*, April 8, 1966.

33. Denver *Post*, March 16, 1966.

34. *Animas–La Plata Project*, "Report of the Commissioner of Reclamation," xii.

35. Dreyfus interview.

36. *Animas–La Plata Project*, "Report of the Commissioner of Reclamation," vi.

37. Ibid., "Comments of the Bureau of the Budget," vii.

38. Reynolds, *Twenty-sixth Biennial Report* and Reynolds interview.

39. *Lower Colorado River Basin Project*, hearings, ibid., 1966, 1205.

40. Reynolds, *Twenty-seventh Biennial Report*, July 1, 1964, to June 30, 1966, 56.

41. Hale interview.

42. *Lower Colorado River Basin Project*, hearings, ibid., 1966, 1209.

43. Ibid.

44. Telephone conversation with Phil Mutz, New Mexico Interstate Stream Commission, engineer, July 25, 1969.

45. *Central Arizona Project*, hearings before the Subcommittee on Water and Power Resources of the Committee on Interior and Insular Affairs, United States Senate, Ninetieth Congress, First Session, 1967, 168.

46. Grand Junction *Daily Sentinel*, undated clipping from the Jeffrey Ingram, southwest representative of the Sierra Club, files on the Colorado River Basin Act.

47. *Twenty-first Annual Report of the Arizona Interstate Stream Commission*, July 1, 1967, to June 30, 1968, 8.

48. Ibid., quotation from a Tucson *Daily Citizen* interview with Aspinall, 13.

49. M. K. U. files, memorandum from Rich Johnson on a meeting with Felix Sparks, August 9, 1967.

50. *Twenty-first Annual Report* of the AISC, 61.

Chapter 6

1. Interview with Morris K. Udall, May 26, 1969.

2. The special master's draft report, May 5, 1960, printed as a part of the record in *Lower Colorado River Basin Project*, hearing before the Subcommittee on Irrigation and Reclamation of the Committee on Interior and Insular Affairs, House of Representatives, Eighty-ninth Congress, First Session, 1965, 399.

3. The decree of the Supreme Court, paragraph 4, March 9, 1964, printed as a part of the record in ibid., 379.

4. Letter from John E. Madden, special counsel, Arizona Interstate Stream Commission, to Congressman Udall, August 26, 1965, printed as a part of the record in ibid., 404.

5. Interview with S. E. Reynolds, May 8, 1969.

6. S. E. Reynolds, *Twenty-sixth Biennial Report of the State Engineer of New Mexico*, July 1, 1962, to June 30, 1964, 117.

7. Joint statement by Claude S. Mann, legal advisor, New Mexico Interstate Stream

Commission, and S. E. Reynolds, secretary, New Mexico Interstate Stream Commission, printed as a part of the record in *Lower Colorado River Basin Project*, hearing, ibid., 1965, 376.

8. Morris K. Udall files on the Central Arizona Project, memorandum on the New Mexico position, recorded October 25, 1963.

9. Reynolds interview.

10. Interview with Claude Wood, administrative assistant to Senator Anderson, May 22, 1969.

11. Interview with Morris K. Udall, May 26, 1969.

12. Interview with Jerry Verkler, May 22, 1969.

13. Udall interview.

14. M. K. U. files, letter from Riney Salmon, Arizona Interstate Stream Commission, to Senator Hayden, October 11, 1963.

15. M. K. U. files, memorandum for the files, April 12, 1964.

16. Udall interview.

17. *Lower Colorado River Basin Project*, hearing, ibid., 1965, 393–97.

18. Ibid., 390–93.

19. Ibid., 388.

20. Ibid., 397.

21. Udall interview.

22. M. K. U. files, joint press release by Congressmen Udall, Rhodes, and George F. Senner, Jr., May 14, 1966.

23. M. K. U. files, memorandum from Congressmen Rhodes and Udall to Senator Anderson on the discussion relative to Hooker Dam, April 26, 1966.

24. M. K. U. files, memorandum for the files, April 29, 1966, and principles of a proposed Arizona–New Mexico agreement, May 17, 1966.

25. M. K. U. files, letter from Senator Anderson to Congressman Udall, May 12, 1966.

26. M. K. U. files, settlement paraphrased from the memorandum sent by Congressmen Rhodes, Udall, and Senner to Senator Anderson, May 12, 1966.

27. *Lower Colorado River Basin Project*, hearings before the Subcommittee on Irrigation and Reclamation of the Committee on Interior and Insular Affairs, House of Representatives, Eighty-ninth Congress, Second Session, 1966, 1202.

28. Ibid., 1208.

29. Ibid., 1211.

30. M. K. U. files, letter from Senator Anderson to Congressman Udall in which Anderson quotes from a letter written him by Mr. Reynolds, May 26, 1966.

31. M. K. U. files, proposed amendments to H.R. 4671, New Mexico draft, May 23, 1966.

32. M. K. U. files, letter from Morris K. Udall to S.E. Reynolds, June 2, 1966.

33. M. K. U. files, letter from Morris K. Udall to Stewart Udall, June 13, 1966.

34. Verkler interview.

35. Udall interview.

36. M. K. U. files, joint statement made by Congressmen Rhodes, Udall, and Senner, an assessment of the status of H.R. 4671, May 21, 1966.

Chapter 7

1. *Lower Colorado River Basin Project*, hearing before the Subcommittee on Irriga-

tion and Reclamation of the Committee on Interior and Insular Affairs, House of Representatives, Eighty-ninth Congress, First Session, 1965, 907.

2. Ibid., 905.

3. *Central Arizona Project*, hearings before the Subcommittee on Water and Power Resources of the Committee on Interior and Insular Affairs, United States Senate, Ninetieth Congress, First Session, 1967, 702.

4. Interview with George Alderson, volunteer worker for the Wilderness Society, who had talked to Mr. Wood and helped to formulate the Wilderness Society position, May 23, 1969.

5. Interview with John Saylor, congressman from Pennsylvania, May 26, 1969.

6. *Central Arizona Project*, hearings, ibid., 446.

7. Ibid., 463.

8. Silver City (N.Mex.) *Daily Press*, June 16, 1967.

9. Jeffrey Ingram files on the Colorado River Basin Act, correspondences from Zeller to Reynolds.

10. *Central Arizona Project*, hearings, ibid., statement by Alvin Franks, president, Hooker Dam Association, 400.

11. Jeffrey Ingram files, letter from Ingram to Anderson, December 14, 1967.

12. Ibid., letter from Ingram to John Young, October 18, 1966.

13. *Central Arizona Project*, hearings, ibid., 399.

14. Ibid., 728–36.

15. Results of a May 1969 questionnaire sent to ten prominent supporters of Hooker Dam in the local area.

16. *Central Arizona Project*, hearings, ibid., 730.

17. May 1969 questionnaire.

18. Jeffrey Ingram files, letter from Franks to Ingram, December 30, 1967.

19. *Central Arizona Project*, hearings, ibid., statement by Senator Anderson, 252.

20. Silver City *Daily Press*, March 26, 1968.

21. Jeffrey Ingram files, letter from Reynolds to Ingram, January 26, 1966.

22. Interview with S. E. Reynolds, May 8, 1969.

23. *Central Arizona Project*, hearings, ibid., 196–97.

24. Jeffrey Ingram files, letter from Anderson to Robert Ingram, August 29, 1967.

25. Ibid., letter from Anderson to an unidentified correspondent, June 28, 1967.

26. Ibid., letter from Anderson to L.C. Victors, October 4, 1967.

27. *Central Arizona Project*, hearings, ibid., 196.

28. Jeffrey Ingram files, letter from Anderson to Jeffrey Ingram, December 4, 1967.

29. Ibid., letter from Anderson to Zeller, May 31, 1967.

30. Interview with Claude Wood, May 22, 1969.

31. *Central Arizona Project*, hearings, ibid., 2.

32. *Albuquerque Journal*, May 14, 1968.

33. *Central Arizona Project*, hearings, ibid., 198.

34. Ibid., 195.

35. Ibid., 393.

36. Interview with William Van Ness and Daniel Dreyfus, staff members of the Senate Interior and Insular Affairs Committee, May 23, 1969.

37. *Congressional Record*, August 7, 1967, S 11048 and August 23, 1967, S 12113.

38. Silver City *Daily Press*, June 26, 1967.

39. Jeffrey Ingram files, memorandum, December 28, 1967.

40. Morris K. Udall files on the Central Arizona Project, memorandum from Verkler to Udall, October 3, 1967.

41. *Lower Colorado River Basin Project*, hearings, ibid., Ninetieth Congress, Second Session, 1968, 822-32.

42. M. K. U. files, letter from Udall to John McComb, Arizona Hiking Club.

43. Ibid., Udall memorandum, October 3, 1967.

44. Ibid., Udall memorandum on conversation with Verkler, October 11, 1967.

45. Interview with Jerry Verkler, May 22, 1969, and Silver City *Daily Press*, February 29, 1968.

46. Jeffrey Ingram files, memorandum from Ingram to Edgar Wayburn, president of the Sierra Club, March 26, 1968, and Silver City *Daily Press*, March 14, 1968.

47. *Colorado River Basin Project, Report and Dissenting Views*, Report No. 1312, House of Representatives, Ninetieth Congress, Second Session.

48. Alderson interview.

49. Interview with Thomas Foley, May 22, 1969.

50. Saylor interview.

51. M. K. U. files, letters from Udall to Sid McFarland, staff director, House Interior and Insular Affairs Committee, March 26 and April 11, 1968.

52. Reynolds interview.

53. Ibid.

54. Jeffrey Ingram files, telegram from Brower to Saylor, May 9, 1968.

55. *Congressional Record*, May 14, 1968, 3880.

56. Ibid., 3881.

57. Dreyfus and Van Ness interview.

58. *Congressional Record*, May 14, 1968, 3880.

59. Saylor interview.

Chapter 9

1. Richard de Uriarte, "Cliff Dam: Arizona Delegation Loses," *Phoenix Gazette*, January 22, 1987.

2. Gary Weatherford, ed., *Water and Agriculture in the Western U.S.: Conservation, Reallocation, and Markets* (Boulder: Westview Press, 1980), 157.

3. Ibid.

4. Ibid., 58.

5. F. Lee Brown and Helen M. Ingram, *Water and Poverty in the Southwest* (Tucson: University of Arizona Press, 1987).

6. Ibid.

7. Uriarte, January 22, 1987, *Phoenix Gazette*.

8. Arizona Department of Water Resources, "Options for Funding Plan 6, a Report to the Arizona Congressional Delegation, January 1985.

9. James C. Decker, "Cost Sharing on Colorado River Water Projects: Upper vs. Lower Basin Perspectives." Prepared for delivery at the 1985 annual meeting of the Western Political Science Association, Las Vegas, March 28-30, 1985.

10. Helen Monberg, *Western Water Resources Wrap Up*, Series XXV, No. 26, June 25, 1987.

11. James C. Decker, "Cost Sharing on Colorado River Water Projects: Upper vs. Lower Basin Perspectives." Paper presented to Western Political Science Association, Las Vegas, March 28-30, 1985.

12. Ibid., 1.

13. Ellen Haddow, "Animas–La Plata Faces Vote," *Rocky Mountain News*, December 7, 1987.

14. Ann Schmidt, "Animas–La Plata Water Project Advances: Narrows Put on Hold," *Denver Post*, May 23, 1985.

15. Helene C. Monberg, "Animas–La Plata Settlement," *Western Resources Wrap Up*, Series XXV, No. 27, July 3, 1986.

16. Haddow, "Battle Over Water Project Continues to Brew," *Rocky Mountain News*, June 1, 1986.

17. "Reagan Signs Water Project Settlement: Animas–La Plata Flows Free of Negotiations Logjam," *Albuquerque Journal*, November 5, 1988.

18. Sandra Griffin, "Minnow Jeopardizes Connor Dam," *El Paso Times*, July 11, 1986.

19. "Smaller Dam Might Replace Connor," *El Paso Times*, September 26, 1986.

20. "Proposed Dam No Threat to Minnows, Board Rules," *Albuquerque Journal*, March 31, 1988.

21. S. E. Reynolds, telephone interview, August 16, 1988.

Index

accommodation, political, 116–17;
  mutual, 32, 38
Active Groundwater Management
  Areas (AMAs), 6, 16–17, 126
activists, conservationist, 98–103
activists, political, 121; Arizona, 44,
  56–57, 59, 82, 88–95; and CAP,
  115–16; Colorado, 74–76, 80–82;
  core, 118; and CRBA, 47–50;
  locally oriented, 118–19, 121; New
  Mexico, 86–96; and policy making,
  31, 34–36. *See also names of
  individuals*
actors, political: behavior of, 96; and
  CRBA, 47–49; involvement of, 34;
  and policy making, 30–31; and
  pork barrel benefits, 15; and water
  development, 10, 118
administrators, water, 10
advertisements, conservationists' use
  of, 55, 101–2, 109
agencies, federal, 14; and water
  development, 9; and water
  marketing, 22–23; and water
  policy, 7
agribusiness, 7, 18
agriculturalists: in Arizona, 46; rural,
  18; and value of water, 5; and
  water development, 9. *See also*
  farmers
agriculture: irrigated, 24; and water
  development, 7, 71–72; and water
  policy, 8; and water rights, 17–18
Agua Fria River, 126
Albuquerque, N.Mex., 17
Albuquerque Journal, 88
allocation, of water, 78; control of, 10;
  efficiency of, 5; and environmentalists, 24; to Indians, 124; study
  of, 52; and water policy, 3, 12. *See
  also* entitlement, water
Allott, Gordon, 63–64, 80–82; and

CRBA, 60; quoted, 109
ALPP. *See* Animas–La Plata Project
AMAs. *See* Active Groundwater
  Management Areas
amendments: to ALPP, 80; Connor,
  111–14; to Hooker Dam proposal,
  110; to Supreme Court decree,
  93–94
analysis: ends-means, 38; method of,
  120. *See also* evaluation
Anderson, Clinton P., 10, 12, 69; and
  ALPP, 79–80; as conservationist,
  101; and CRBA, 50, 52–53, 57; and
  Gila controversy, 87–89, 91–96; and
  Hooker Dam, 100, 102, 104–15;
  influence of, 118, 120; quoted,
  106–7; retirement of, 129
Anderson, Raymond L., 6
Andrus, Cecil, 124
Animas–La Plata Project (ALPP), 4,
  26–27, 84, 87, 119, 122; authorization of, 66–83; implementation of,
  123, 127–29, 129–32; political
  feasibility of, 116–17; rescue of, 22
Animas River, 26, 68
apportionment of Gila River water,
  84, 96
Appropriations Committee: House,
  10, 129; Senate, 47, 61
Appropriations Subcommittee on
  Public Works, House, 47
aqueduct, Tucson, 125, 132
aquifers: Arizona, 46; demands on, 7;
  safe yield for, 6, 16
arenas, policy-making, 7, 23, 31, 36–37,
  131
aridity, acceptance of, 25
Arizona: and commitment to CAP, 91,
  123; and CRBA, 26–27, 43–48, 72;
  and Gila controversy, 84; groundwater reform act in, 16; policy
  making in, 24; water allotted to,

145

Index

Mulholland, William, 10
municipalities: in Arizona, 46;
  influence of, 124; water demands
  of, 17; and water market, 16–17;
  and water policy, 7
Mutz, Phil, 94

National Environmental Policy Act
  (1969), 15
national interest, and conservation,
  114–15
National Mine Workers Union, 56
national parks, preservation of, 7, 12,
  101
National Park Service, 69
national park system, 55
National Water Commission, 3, 16, 60,
  63, 78, 110
natural resources, development of, 52
natural systems, modification of, 7
nature, and water supply, 17
Navajo Dam, 71
Navajo Generating Station, 123
Navajo Indian Irrigation Project, 12
negotiations, Arizona–New Mexico,
  90–95, 97. See also bargaining,
  political; compromise; consent
  building; majority building
Nevada, 27, 74; and CRBA, 48, 72;
  water allotted to, 54
Newlands Act, 20
New Mexico, 118; and ALPP, 67,
  69–71, 73, 78–80, 82–83, 128; and
  CRBA, 8, 43, 48, 54–55, 58, 72; and
  Gila controversy, 84–96, 117, 121;
  and Hooker Dam, 97; water
  projects in, 4, 26–30, 129
New Mexico Game and Fish Commission, 130
New Mexico Interstate Stream
  Commission, 79, 121
New Mexico Wildlife Federation, 98
newspapers, 75–76; and CAP, 45, 123;
  and CRBA, 61. See also names of
  newspapers
New York Times, 55–56
Nichols, John, The Milagro Beanfield
  War, 12
Non-Intercourse Act, 19
noninterference, mutual, 38–39,
  40–41, 96, 110, 114, 119–20; erosion
  of, 132; inadequacy of, 122
noninvolvement, 96; and Hooker

Dam controversy, 109
Northwest, 33; and CRBA, 52; and
  interbasin transfer, 58

objectives, of water policy, 2, 33, 41–42
Office of Management and Budget
  (OMB), 53, 74, 127; and water
  policy, 35, 130. See also Bureau of
  the Budget
OMB. See Office of Management and
  Budget
opinion formulation, 120–21
opposition: to Grand Canyon dams,
  98; to Hooker Dam, 97–103,
  105–15. See also conflict
Orme, John, 10
Orme Dam, 124–26
overdevelopment, impact of, 6–7
overdrafts, water, 6, 12; elimination
  of, 124; groundwater, 7, 124
overexploitation, 24–25
overuse, consequences of, 11
Owens Valley, 10
ownership, of water, 18–19, 32–33

Pacific Southwest Water Plan
  (PSWWP), 27, 48–49, 54, 88
packages, congressional, 38–39, 41,
  80; development of, 52, 47–49,
  57–58, 60, 62–63
Parker Dam, 28, 43
participants, in policy making, 7–8, 12,
  22–24. See also activists, political;
  actors, political
patterns, political, 2–5, 13, 31, 82, 120;
  of future water policy, 121–22
Paulek, Victor, quoted, 67
Peabody Coal Company, 77
perceptions, of water issues, 120–22
Peripheral Canal, 17, 24
petition, supporting ALPP, 67
Phoenix, Ariz., 16, 17, 26, 49, 126–27
Pima-Maricopa Indians, 89, 126
Place No One Knew, The, 11
policy: analysis, 3–4; decisions, 6;
  design, consequences of, 24
policy-making process, 2, 12, 22,
  30–42; congressional, 118–19. See
  also titles of legislation
political feasibility: of CRBA, 59;
  importance of, 116–19; and policy
  making, 30–42, 122, 123; and
  water development, 9